Praying the Roman Missal

Pastoral Reflections on the Revised English Translation

Reverend Robert L. Tuzik, PHD

LITURGY
TRAINING
PUBLICATIONS

Nihil Obstat
Very Reverend Daniel A. Smilanic, JCD
Vicar for Canonical Services
Archdiocese of Chicago
May 31, 2011

Imprimatur
Reverend Monsignor John F. Canary, STL, DMIN
Vicar General
Archdiocese of Chicago
May 31, 2011

Cover and interior image © The Crosiers/Gene Plaisted, OSC

Printed in the United States of America.

Library of Congress Control Number: 2011932513

ISBN 978-1-56854-923-1

PRM

Contents

Preface

As a liturgical consultant to His Eminence Francis Cardinal George, OMI, Archbishop of Chicago, I have had the privilege of reviewing numerous proposals considered for the English translation of the third edition of *The Roman Missal*. As consultant to the Congregation for Divine Worship and the Discipline of the Sacraments (CDWDS), the Vox Clara Subcommittee of CDWDS, and the International Commission on English in the Liturgy (ICEL), I have learned a great deal about the challenges involved in producing the final translation of the third edition of *The Roman Missal*.

When I hear and read comments about the revised translation, I often hear people talking about problems they have with individual words, grammatical structures, and ease of proclamation. While I wholeheartedly recognize that this new text is not a perfect translation, I also believe that we are in danger of losing an important perspective when we focus too much on individual words, phrases, and clauses. For ultimately what we are talking about is liturgical prayer. Will the revised translation of the third edition of *The Roman Missal* help us to pray as a community of faith?

I titled this book *Praying the Roman Missal: Pastoral Reflections on the Revised English Translation*. In our catechesis preparing people to use the third edition of *The Roman Missal*, we must focus on the fact that we are talking about liturgical prayer. In fact, we are talking about the highest level of prayer that we can experience, since the prayers in *The Roman Missal* are used at the celebration of the Eucharist. What is the value of liturgical prayer, and how does it differ from private prayer?

The *Constitution on the Sacred Liturgy*, 7, reminds us that "the liturgy is considered as an exercise of the priestly office of Jesus Christ. In the liturgy, by means of signs perceptible to the senses, human sanctification is signified and brought about in ways proper to each of these signs; in the liturgy the whole public worship is performed by the Mystical Body of Jesus Christ, that is, by the Head and his members. From this it follows that every liturgical celebration, because it is an action of Christ the Priest and of his Body which is the Church, is a sacred action surpassing all others; no other action of the Church can equal its effectiveness by the same title and to the same degree." This would include private prayer.

Many years ago, Saint John Vianney explained the superiority of liturgical prayer in these words: "Private prayer is like straw scattered here and there. If you set it on fire, it makes a lot of little flames. But gather these straws into a bundle and light them, and you get a mighty fire, rising like a column into the sky; public prayer is like that."[1] Liturgical prayer is a public expression and formation of the spirituality (self-identity) of the Church. As such, it helps us to hear the voice of God speaking to us in Word and Sacrament and then to respond by our entrance into a deeper communion with God and others.

Prayer is indeed one of God's greatest gifts to us. Prayer is the gift of an ability to respond to God so that we might enter into an experience of communion (loving union) with God and his people. The essence of any prayer experience is the experience of loving communion with God and others. The words, the songs, the gestures, the use of material objects, standing, sitting, keeping silence are all means to an end: the experience of communion. If you have to have an ultimate criterion by which you measure your time spent in prayer, ask yourself this question: How strong was my experience of communion with God and others?

In his apostolic exhortation *The Sacrament of Charity* (*Sacramentum Caritatis* [SC]), Pope Benedict XVI challenges us to make our whole life an act of worship. As Pope Benedict says in article 16: "The Church *receives* and at the same time *expresses*

---

1 Leonard Foley, Ed., *Saint of the Day, 5th Revised Edition*, Cincinnati: St. Anthony Messenger Press, 2003, p. 191.

what she herself is in the seven sacraments, thanks to which God's grace concretely influences the lives of the faithful, so that their whole existence, redeemed by Christ, can become an act of worship pleasing to God (SC, 16). In fact, this is what Eucharistic Prayer IV refers to, when it asks God to grant that all who partake of the one bread and one chalice "may truly become a living sacrifice in Christ / to the praise of your glory."

In his apostolic letter *Spiritus et Sponsa: On the 40th Anniversary of the Constitution on the Sacred Liturgy, Sacrosanctum Concilium*, 12, Pope John Paul II affirms the importance of our efforts to celebrate the liturgy:

> The Liturgy offers the deepest and most effective answer to this yearning for the encounter with God. It does so especially in the Eucharist, in which we are given to share in the sacrifice of Christ and to nourish ourselves with his Body and his Blood. However, Pastors must ensure that the sense of mystery penetrates consciences, making them rediscover the *art of "mystagogic catechesis,"* so dear to the Fathers of the Church. It is their duty, in particular, to promote dignified celebrations, paying the proper attention to the different categories of persons: children, young people, adults, the elderly, the disabled. They must all feel welcome at our gatherings, so that they may breathe the atmosphere of the first community of believers who "devoted themselves to the Apostles' teaching and fellowship, to the breaking of bread and the prayers" (Acts 2:42).

Therefore, we need to ask ourselves: How effective are our liturgical celebrations in fostering a loving communion with God and others?

If we are to be successful in preparing people to pray with the third edition of *The Roman Missal*, then we need to set our reception of this new translation in the context of what it means for our prayer life. Will the new translation be an effective expression and formation of what it means to be the Church? Will it lead to the sanctification of the lives of the people participating in the liturgy? Will it give a new and more powerful voice to God, who speaks to us and nourishes us in Word and Sacrament in every liturgical celebration? Will this new translation eventually become a comfortable and inspiring way for English-speaking Catholics to enter into a profound experience of mystery, of loving communion with God and each other?

In *Praying the Roman Missal*, I will explain the various parts of the revised Missal in terms of the ways in which a successful implementation of the third edition of *The Roman Missal* can be a very positive help to our participation in the liturgical prayer and life of the Church. I am personally convinced that during this preparation period there is a great potential for good, both corporate and personal, if we only approach the use of the revised Missal with an open mind.

I envision this book as a resource for various groups in the parish, whose influence will enable the parish at large to give the new translation the time it needs in order to prove itself an effective mediator of our corporate experience of God in our midst. I hope this book will answer the types of questions that you can expect from the leaders of the local community.

In particular, I have written this book to appeal to parish councils, school boards, religious education boards, Catholic school teachers, catechists, RCIA teams, liturgy committees, musicians, cantors, and choir members. At the same time, this guidebook can also serve as a good, all-in-one introduction for parishioners desiring to read one book that covers the various parts of *The Roman Missal*. In short, I hope this book will provide a general and comprehensive overview of a very important prayer book that will profoundly influence the growth of our faith for many years to come.

Reverend Robert L. Tuzik, PHD

Chapter 1
Translating *The Roman Missal* into English

Since the conclusion of the Second Vatican Council on December 8, 1965, we have had three typical editions of *The Roman Missal* in Latin, which have been translated into English by the International Commission on English in the Liturgy (ICEL). ICEL is considered a mixed commission, composed of several episcopal conferences that use the English language for worship. ICEL was founded on October 17, 1963, since the decision had already been made by the Bishops at the Second Vatican Council to allow the public celebration of the Mass and the sacraments in the vernacular.

On December 4, 1963, Pope Paul VI promulgated the *Constitution on the Sacred Liturgy (Sacrosanctum Concilium)*. The idea of translating *The Roman Missal* into the vernacular is found in article 25 of the *Constitution*: "The liturgical books are to be revised as soon as possible; experts are to be employed on the task and bishops from various parts of the world are to be consulted." Article 36.4 states: "Translations from the Latin text into the mother tongue intended for use in the liturgy must be approved by the competent, territorial ecclesiastical authority already mentioned."

As a result of these goals, those territories where English is used by a significant proportion of the Catholic people joined ICEL to prepare English translations of the Latin liturgical books, which the various member episcopal conferences could vote on prior to seeking final approval from Rome. Full membership in

ICEL is held by those episcopal conferences that have substantial numbers of people desiring to celebrate the liturgy in English: Australia, Canada, England and Wales, India, Ireland, New Zealand, Pakistan, the Philippines, Scotland, South America, and the United States of America.

In addition to the full members, there are numerous episcopal conferences that celebrate Mass and the sacraments in English among other languages. These episcopal conferences comprise the associate members of ICEL: Antilles, Bangladesh, CEPAC (Episcopal Conference of the Pacific), Gambia-Liberia-Sierra Leone, Ghana, Kenya, Malaysia-Singapore, Malawi, Nigeria, Papua New Guinea and the Solomons, Sri Lanka, Tanzania, Uganda, Zambia, and Zimbabwe. In other words, the influence of ICEL and its English translation of the liturgy is worldwide.

In 1969, the first edition of the Order of Mass of *The Roman Missal* in English was published. ICEL was rushed into producing an English translation due to the surge of enthusiasm among the people to experience a vernacular liturgy. In this process, some of the connections with scripture, with the homilies of the Fathers of the Church, and with the poetry and rhythm of the Latin language were lost.

In 1974, the complete edition of *The Roman Missal* in English was issued. It was more complete than the first edition. The first edition needed to be revised in accord with the documents and directives issued since the publication of the first edition—that is, the June 29, 1970, *Instruction on the Extension of Distributing Holy Communion under Both Kinds* and the September 5, 1970, *Third Instruction on the Correct Implementation of the Constitution on the Sacred Liturgy*. However, much of the translation of the second edition of *The Roman Missal* was the same as the rushed translation of the first edition.

Too often the 1974 translation simply paraphrased the Latin text, losing much of the richness of metaphor and imagery found in the original. Creative additions in English were still to be found in this edition. Superficial contemporary expressions and phrases robbed the Roman liturgy of its richness. The truly sacred language of the Roman liturgy seemed to be lost by the more secular usages that were employed. Very often, people complained of a loss of the awe and mystery that the celebration of the liturgy should engender in people. Since liturgy is formative of our Catholic faith (the Latin principle of *lex orandi, lex credendi*), we need to develop a liturgical language in the vernacular that captures the sacredness and poetry of the Latin text.

In 2002, the third edition of *The Roman Missal* (*Missale Romanum, editio typica tertia*) was promulgated by Pope John Paul II. More than 15 percent of the texts are new, due to the large number of new saints canonized by Pope John Paul II and requests for texts to address special circumstances (e.g., wedding anniversaries). Since 2002, major efforts have been made to translate this third typical edition of *The Roman Missal* into English. The new translation has been guided by several new decrees, which have addressed the questions raised by our Bishops and their consultants regarding the norms for translating Latin into English.

When ICEL began the work of translating the first edition of *The Roman Missal* into English, very general guidelines were given to them in the documents of Vatican II and in post-conciliar Instructions such as the September 26, 1964, *Instruction of the Sacred Congregation of Rites on Putting into Effect the Constitution on the Sacred Liturgy* (*Inter Oecumenici*, Article XI: Translations of liturgical texts into the language of the people). On January 25, 1969, the Consilium charged with implementing the decrees of Vatican II issued the Instruction *Comme le prévoit (Instruction on the Translation of Liturgical Texts for Celebrations with a Congregation)*. This Instruction is often known by its French title, since the initial working draft was written in French.

Dynamic Equivalence

One of the theories that prevailed among the translators used by
ICEL was that of dynamic equivalence. ICEL wanted to convey
the meaning of the Latin text by using the dynamic equivalent, in
modern-day words and metaphors, of what the Latin text says literally. This led them to add explanatory words not found in the
Latin or to delete images that they thought were unnecessary. For
example, some Latin prayers refer to an angel standing before
God's throne holding a golden censer with clouds of incense rising
before God. ICEL eliminated the reference to the angel in favor of
a simpler translation which spoke only of the incense rising before
God's throne. As a result of the theory of dynamic equivalence,
ICEL often departed from a more literal approach to translation.

Call for New Texts

Another problem ICEL had to deal with was the call for the creation of new texts not found in the Latin version of *The Roman
Missal* in order to meet contemporary needs. A good example of
this is the creation of new Collects for special circumstances (for
example, "For One Who Died Suddenly" or "For a Child Who
Died before Baptism"). Another example was the call for more variety in the liturgy, answered by creating new Eucharistic Prayers.

ICEL also addressed pressing issues such as the call to use
inclusive language, avoiding language which some contemporary
Catholics view as excluding females (for example, the frequent
use of "men" to refer to both men and women). The question of
liturgical inculturation was also hotly debated. How much adap-
tation of the Roman liturgy is permissible in order to honor the
customs and traditions of different racial and ethnic groups? If
the liturgy is inserted into the culture, tradition, and history of
the people celebrating it, then how does this insertion affect our
judgment as to what constitutes an accurate translation of our
prayer tradition? What values does a translation need to preserve
in order to transmit faithfully the essentials of our Catholic faith?

LITURGIAM AUTHENTICAM

These issues were finally addressed when the Congregation for Divine Worship and the Discipline of the Sacraments (CDWDS) issued the *Fifth Instruction for the Right Implementation of the Constitution on the Sacred Liturgy of the Second Vatican Council.* This Instruction is known by its Latin title, *Liturgiam authenticam* (*On the Use of Vernacular Languages in the Publication of the Books of the Roman Liturgy*). This Instruction was approved by Pope John Paul II on March 20, 2001, and took effect on April 25, 2001.

The new norms in *Liturgiam authenticam* supersede all norms previously set forth on liturgical translation, with the exception of those in the *Fourth Instruction on the Right Implementation of the Constitution on the Sacred Liturgy* (*Varietates Legitimae*), which dealt with inculturation. *Liturgiam authenticam* explains the considerations that need to be taken in producing a modern vernacular translation of a liturgical text:

- Preserve biblical references by referring to the Neo-Vulgate, the current Catholic version of the Latin Bible.
- Avoid exaggerated dependence on modern modes of expression and psychologizing language.
- Strive to use inclusive language whenever possible without resorting to cumbersome constructions in English that hinder the legitimate use of nouns and pronouns capable of referring to both the masculine and the feminine in a single term.
- Maintain the traditional grammatical gender of the Trinity (Father, Son, Holy Spirit).
- Translate expressions such as "Son of Man" and the "Fathers of the Church" exactly as found in biblical and liturgical texts.
- Do not extend or restrict the meaning of the original term used in Latin.
- Avoid using any terms that recall publicity slogans or those that have political, ideological, or similar overtones.

- Maintain continuity as much as possible between the original and vernacular texts.
- Aim to create a language with a distinctive liturgical style suitable for worship, in accord with popular Catholic usage and major catechetical texts.
- Translate literally words referring to figurative language, for example, the "finger," the "hand," the "face" of God, or of God "walking" among us, etc.
- Maintain distinctive features that incorporate biblical imagery.
- Develop a dignified vernacular liturgy for worship.
- Attend to matters of syntax, style, and literary genre.
- Maintain relationships between clauses, parallel constructions, distinctive terms, and metaphors found in the Latin text.
- Attend to the ease of public proclamation when a text is read aloud or sung.

Liturgiam authenticam also contained specific norms regarding the translation of Eucharistic Prayers and the Creed (for example, the return to "I believe" to translate the Latin word *Credo*), provided clarifications of the process of translation to be followed, and highlighted the need for obtaining approval, the *recognitio*, from Rome prior to the use of any text.

While *Liturgiam authenticam* was very comprehensive, our Bishops and ICEL still had questions on translating specific words, phrases, and metaphors used in the Latin text. There was need for even greater explanation of the rationale or principles of translation along with some concrete examples.

RATIO TRANSLATIONIS

In 2005, the CDWDS issued a working draft of the *Ratio translationis* for the English language. The *Ratio translationis* presents the process and principles of translation. The *Ratio* consists of three parts.

Part I, "Presuppositions for the Authentic Translation of Liturgical Texts in the Roman Rite," covers the meaning of liturgical language, the main characteristics of the language of the Roman Rite, including its patristic origins, and the gradual organic development of a "liturgical vernacular."

Part II, "Principles of Translation for the Liturgy of the Roman Rite," is divided into subsections: "Identity and Unitary Expression of the Roman Rite," "Adaptations to the Qualities and Exigencies of the Vernacular Language," and the "Oral-Aural-Mnemonic Dimensions of Translation."

Part III, "Application of the Principles of Translation to the English Language," concerns style, syntax, genre, person, number, and gender of words, plus the translation of Greek and Hebrew terms.

With the final approval of the *Ratio translationis* by the Holy Father in 2006, Rome addressed a great number of the issues that have been raised over the years since Vatican II regarding the vernacular translation of the Latin liturgy. Often, our current translation has been criticized for being bland, eliminating metaphors found in the Latin text, weakening or obscuring biblical and patristic references, not translating all the words in Latin, adding unnecessary explanatory words not found in the Latin text, changing the meaning of the Latin text, and creating new texts not found in the Latin *editio typica*. A stricter, more literal approach to translation was developed that addressed the above issues and worked to implement the recommendations and guidelines found in *Liturgiam authenticam* and the *Ratio translationis*.

What is the process that our Bishops have followed in producing a vernacular translation of *The Roman Missal* that they can submit to Rome for final approval? While the process is quite complex, the general lines are fairly easy to explain.

When our Bishops request that ICEL provide a new translation of the Latin *editio typica* for one of our liturgical books, the executive committee of Bishops who meet monthly and supervise the work of ICEL submits to the episcopal board the names of the members of a translation committee, who will develop a preliminary translation. The board selects qualified individuals from the various nations that make up ICEL to serve on the translation committees. These individuals are experts in Latin, patristics, the Bible, linguistics, philology, poetry, and music.

A base translator, who has received a *Nihil Obstat* from the CDWDS, prepares a literal translation of the Latin text as a point of reference for evaluating any translations submitted by members of the translation committee. In addition, one or more of ICEL's approved list of consultants provides one possible translation for the translation committee to review in order to come up with a text that they will submit to the episcopal board for review and approval. Usually, an ad hoc revision committee appointed by the executive committee evaluates the proposed text for its fidelity, exactness, and appropriateness for oral procla-mation. At least one Bishop from ICEL is a part of the ad hoc revision committee. If a Bishop dissents from the recommenda-tions of the revision committee, a summary of his reasons for doing so is also communicated to the conferences by ICEL along with the draft translation.

Once the episcopal board has approved a tentative text, a draft known as the Green Book is published and submitted to the various episcopal conferences for review and a preliminary consultative vote (using the threefold classification: it pleases, it does not please, or it pleases with reservations). In addition to consulting with its own experts, the episcopal board also has the option of seeking the assistance of the CDWDS in reviewing its preliminary text, to avoid encountering any big problems once a final text is submitted for approval.

The CDWDS has a subcommittee known as Vox Clara, which reviews parts of the preliminary translations that our Bishops are considering. Vox Clara ("Clear Voice") is composed of senior Bishops, some of whom are members of the CDWDS. ICEL has found the recommendations of Vox Clara to be most helpful in its deliberations regarding the suitability of the translation of particular texts and the amount of freedom ICEL has regarding its implementation of the recommendations found in *Liturgiam authenticam* and the *Ratio translationis.*

The ICEL staff then collates the feedback received from the various episcopal conferences, the CDWDS, Vox Clara, and a large group of experts whose advice our Bishops have sought in evaluating the Green Book text. *The Roman Missal* editorial committee creates a text that is presented to the episcopal board for approval and emendation. Once the revised text is approved by the episcopal board, it is sent as a draft known as the Grey Book to the various episcopal conferences for approval. Approval of the Grey Book requires a two-thirds majority of all the full members of ICEL. Every episcopal conference retains the right to amend the Grey Book, although these amendments are kept to a minimum. At this stage, any amendments to the Grey Book sought by an episcopal conference are handled individually by the CDWDS. Once ICEL has obtained the approval of two-thirds of the episcopal conferences holding full membership, the Grey Book is sent to CDWDS for approval.

Obtaining Final Approval of the New Translation

CDWDS reviews the text approved by the Bishops' conferences that make up ICEL, makes whatever changes it deems necessary, and then submits the final version of the translation to the Holy Father for approval. Once the approval or *recognitio* of the Holy See is granted, the book is then ready to be sent to publishers who will produce the final, approved version of the liturgical book for distribution and sale to Catholic churches in the English-speaking world. It takes six months to a year to produce a finished product in book form, depending on the length of the text.

Sometimes, people ask why it took so long for the translation of *The Roman Missal* to reach completion. Once you consider all that is involved in producing a new translation in the vernacular, you realize that the number of people to be consulted—local Bishops, Roman officials, episcopal offices of divine worship, CDWDS, Vox Clara, and numerous experts in diverse fields: biblical scholars, professional musicians, parish and religious leaders—is huge.

To reach consensus on a translation that will receive the approval of the member episcopal conferences of ICEL is a time-consuming task. Some episcopal conferences meet only once a year. Many episcopal conferences have voted on the Missal in parts, as soon as ICEL issued a Grey Book version of a section of the Missal. And so, while the finished product is more than 1,000 pages long, the preliminary work in approving parts of the Missal as the translation became available did speed up the likelihood that the final product would be approved.

Everyone associated with the production of the third edition of *The Roman Missal* wants the new translation to be accepted by our people and to be seen as an improvement on what we are now using. While I believe that most people will be happy and comfortable with the new translation, there will always be a few who will find fault with the way certain words, phrases, or sentences were translated.

The English text is meant to accommodate many different English-speaking nations. Therefore, there are bound to be some concerns raised by individual countries regarding the translation. This is why Rome allows individual episcopal conferences to make amendments to the main translation: to provide for the specific linguistic needs of their people. Hopefully, the changes sought by individual episcopal conferences will be few, and a strong sense of unity in prayer will be felt across the English-speaking world once the new edition of *The Roman Missal* is approved and published.

On March 26, 2010, prior to announcing it to the public, His Eminence Francis Cardinal George, OMI, as President of the U.S. Conference of Catholic Bishops (USCCB), received a letter from Rome approving the revised translation. The third edition of *The Roman Missal* was publicly approved by Pope Benedict XVI at the April 28, 2010, meeting of Vox Clara, the subcommittee evaluating the English-language translation of the CDWDS. After some minor editing of the text during the summer (taking care of typos and making sure that the final edition reflects the final changes approved by the Holy Father and the CDWDS), the USCCB received the final text of the third edition of *The Roman Missal* in August of 2010, along with the approved adaptations, proper texts, and calendar for use in the dioceses of the United States of America. The letter containing the *recognitio* was received by Cardinal George on July 24, 2010. The mandatory implementation date for the use of the third edition of *The Roman Missal* was scheduled for the First Sunday of Advent, November 27, 2011.

Translating liturgical texts in Latin into the English language poses many challenges to our Bishops and to ICEL. Is the translation faithful to the Latin original? Is the English translation an excellent literary production in its own right? Can the translation be set to music? Has it preserved the metaphors, scriptural and patristic references, contrasts and comparisons, and imagery of the Latin original? Will it stand the test of time and be accepted by the people? Will it nourish the piety and spiritual sensitivities of peoples from diverse nations who use the English language? Does it successfully address the issues of inclusive language and the needs of inculturation? Does it implement the principles and norms for translation mandated by the CDWDS and the Holy Father?

I hope the preceding essay has cleared up some of the confusion and addressed some of your concerns about the new translation of *The Roman Missal*. We have been waiting a long time. However, I'm confident that once people experience the new translation, most will be satisfied with the new translation of the third typical edition of *The Roman Missal.*

QUESTIONS FOR CONTINUED REFLECTION

1. How many English-speaking nations are part of the International Commission on English in the Liturgy?

2. What problems are posed for ICEL by having so many nations that need a common text acceptable to two-thirds of the member episcopal conferences?

3. What type of guidelines did ICEL receive in the first decade of its existence? Did these guidelines provide adequate guidance for the task of translating the Latin liturgy into English?

4. What is the theory of dynamic equivalence?

5. How strict are the guidelines found in *Liturgiam authenticam* compared to those found in *Comme le prévoit*?

6. What is the *Ratio translationis*?

7. When you hear of the complex process used to produce the final English text of the third edition of *The Roman Missal*, do you feel that adequate consultation took place in creating the revised translation of *The Roman Missal*?

Chapter 2
Proper of Time

The Proper of Time refers to that lengthy section of *The Roman Missal* that deals with the proper Mass to be celebrated at a particular liturgical time. This includes the following times:

1. Advent
2. Christmas Time
3. Lent
4. Holy Week
5. The Sacred Paschal Triduum
6. Easter Time
7. Ordinary Time
8. Solemnities of the Lord during Ordinary Time:
   - The Most Holy Trinity
   - The Most Holy Body and Blood of Christ (*Corpus Christi*)
   - The Most Sacred Heart of Jesus
   - Our Lord Jesus Christ, King of the Universe

In the Proper of Time you will find complete Masses (Collect, Prayer over the Offerings, and Prayer after Communion) for the Sundays and weekdays of that particular liturgical time. The third edition of *The Roman Missal* uses the word "time" in place of the word "season" to describe what we used to call the Christmas season and the Easter season. Of course, we used the title "Ordinary Time" in the previous translation. This did not change.

Where the previous translation referred to the "Proper of Seasons," the new translation more accurately refers to the

"Proper of Time." This may take a while to get used to, but the texts referred to in the eight parts of the Proper of Time are the same texts as in the previous Proper of Seasons, except that the wording of the prayers has been updated and corrected for accuracy.

The Advent season is now referred to simply as Advent. The Lenten season is now referred to simply as Lent. Holy Week continues to be called Holy Week. Where previous editions of *The Sacramentary* spoke of "Passion Sunday (Palm Sunday)," the new translation combines the two titles into one: "Palm Sunday of the Passion of the Lord."

Beginning with Thursday of the Lord's Supper at the Evening Mass, continuing through the Friday of the Passion of the Lord (Good Friday), and culminating in the Easter Vigil in the Holy Night [of Easter] and Easter Sunday of the Resurrection of the Lord—these three days are now referred to as "The Sacred Paschal Triduum," rather than the "Easter Triduum" as in the previous translation. These new titles reflect the emphasis on a more literal, accurate translation of the Latin text.

The previous Proper of Seasons always ended with a section containing the Solemnities of the Lord during Ordinary Time. This tradition continues, with these four Masses grouped together in *The Roman Missal* immediately after the numbered Sunday Masses for Ordinary Time. They are in the same place in *The Roman Missal* as they were in the previous edition of *The Sacramentary*. This did not change.

While the titles may be slightly different, the essential content of the Proper of Time is the same as that found in the previous edition of *The Sacramentary*. Let's look at the various parts of the Proper of Time.

ADVENT

While a complete introduction to the theology of the various times in the Proper of Time is beyond the scope of this book, let me refer the reader to an important decree, which is included in

the front of *The Roman Missal* prior to beginning the texts for
Advent: *The Universal Norms on the Liturgical Year and the General
Roman Calendar.* This decree describes all the constituent parts
of the liturgical year, explaining their purpose and summarizing
their theology. It briefly explains the design of the General
Roman Calendar and summarizes for each month all the feasts
and celebrations approved by the General Roman Calendar during that month.

Of course, every episcopal conference can petition Rome
to add special celebrations on certain days that are not found in
the General Roman Calendar. For example, there is a complete
Mass for Blessed Pope John XXIII in the Italian version of *The
Roman Missal*, but not in the English version.

This book aims to explain the differences in the translation of the prayer texts used throughout the year. It hopes to
evaluate the improvements made in the translation of the Latin
text into English. It aims to describe the rationale behind the
decisions made about the new wording of our prayers. In doing
so, it also criticizes some of the inadequacies of the previous
translation, which the new translation aimed to correct.

Let's look at the Collect of the First Sunday of Advent.
Collects on the first Sundays of a new liturgical time are quite
important in setting a tone for the Masses that are part of that
time.

Previous Translation	New Translation

All-powerful God,
increase our *strength of will*
    for *doing good*
that Christ may find an *eager
    welcome* at his coming
and *call* us to his *side* in the
    kingdom of heaven, . . .
	Grant your faithful, we pray,
	    almighty God,
	the *resolve to run forth to meet
	    your* Christ
	with *righteous deeds* at his
	    coming,
	so that, *gathered* at his *right hand*,
	they may be *worthy to possess* the
	    heavenly Kingdom.

This Collect demonstrates the different approach that the previous translation took with translating the Latin text. I have italicized the words in the previous translation that are either a mistranslation of the Latin text or else new words added by the previous translation which did not adequately convey the meaning of the Latin text. In the new translation, I italicized all of the words that were not accurately translated by the previous translation. This accounts for the differences between the two translations.

The reference to "almighty God" occurs later in the first line in the new translation—the same place where it is found in the Latin text. The previous translation tended to move the reference to God to the very start of the prayer. Often, it changed the reference to "Lord" or "God" to "Father." Latin has more variety in the wording of its prayer texts than the previous translation led you to believe.

"Increase our strength of will for doing good" does miss the rich biblical metaphor found in "Grant your faithful, we pray, almighty God, / the resolve to run forth to meet your Christ." The previous translation does not refer to the people as "your faithful." "Increase our strength" is very different from the metaphor "grant . . . the resolve to run forth." There is a sense of urgency, of anticipation to meet Christ, that is not entirely conveyed in the previous translation. Notice the use of the possessive pronoun "your" before "Christ." "Your Christ" reminds us of the Hebrew meaning behind the word "Christ": the anointed one, the Messiah. Of course, preparing for the coming of the Messiah is a major theme of Advent.

More is intended in the Latin text than simply to pray that God increase our strength of will to do good. The Latin text makes direct reference to meeting Christ (the Messiah) with righteous deeds. "Righteous deeds" better conveys the biblical connection to the Advent theme of reforming our lives by returning to the path of righteousness than the previous translation's use of the more generic "doing good."

The previous translation sounds weaker than the new translation when it refers to Christ to"call us to his side." The new translation correctly translates the Latin text as "gathered at his right hand." While a "call" from God is important, it is not the same as the action of gathering a people into the heavenly Kingdom. Of course, the Latin phrase *eius dexterae sociati* means "gathered at his right hand." The word *dexterae* means "right hand" and is a reference to the same phrase used in both the Nicene Creed and the Apostles' Creed.

The petition that God find the faithful "*worthy to possess the heavenly Kingdom*" (emphasis added) is much stronger than the previous translation's use of Christ calling us "to his side." Don't we hope to be worthy to possess a place in the heavenly Kingdom? There is no substitute for an accurate translation of the Latin.

From the lengthy discussion above, you can see how much is involved in preparing a worthy translation of a Latin text into English. There are so many factors to be considered. While I do not have time to go through more texts from Advent, let me assure you that the types of changes made to the previous translation are both justified and necessary in order to unleash the full beauty and power of our Roman prayer tradition, of which these texts are a part.

Christmas Time

No Collect used during Christmas Time has quite the impact as the beautiful Collect used in the Mass at Midnight. No longer is this Mass called the "Mass at Midnight." Now it is called "At the Mass during the Night." This leaves us with some flexibility about the timing of this Mass. While many people enjoy participating in a traditional Midnight Mass, evening Mass during the Night could be celebrated earlier than midnight in order to accommodate families with little children and older people, who seldom are awake at midnight.

Let's look at the Collect for the "Mass during the Night."

Previous Translation	New Translation

Father,
you make this holy night
    radiant
with the splendor of *Jesus Christ* our light.
We welcome him as *Lord*, the
    true light of the *world*.
Bring us to *eternal* joy in the
    kingdom of heaven, . . .
	O God, who have made this
	    most sacred night
	radiant with the splendor of the
	    true light,
	grant, *we pray*, that we who have
	    known the *mysteries* of his
	    light on *earth*,
	may also *delight* in his gladness
	    in heaven.

One of the hallmarks of the prayers in the Roman Rite is their simplicity, directness, conciseness in expression, and their connection with the rich biblical and patristic tradition upon which they are based. The previous translation all too often gave in to wordiness, adding explanatory texts when no additional words were needed. I italicized all of the words used in the previous translation that are not found in the Latin text.

Very often, the previous translation rendered the Latin word for God (*Deus*) as Father (which actually is the word *Pater* in Latin). The Roman prayers provided a good deal of variety in referring to God. One of the most popular and most direct references to the deity in Roman Collects is simply to say "O God." After all, simplicity is a hallmark of our Roman prayer tradition. In addition, the previous translation frequently did away with the superlative adjectives used in our prayers. Rather than say "this most sacred night," the previous translation says "this holy night." There is something very special about a "most sacred night" that a mere "holy night" does not convey.

All too often, the petition in the prayer is obscured, when the previous translation neglects to translate the words for "grant, we pray." These words are found everywhere in our Roman prayers. Also missing in many of the previous translations is the reference to "mysteries." The temptation was to explain the "mystery" as though we could really explain in a few words the meaning of a mystery. The new translation restores the reference to "mysteries of his light on earth."

The new translation also appeals to our affective sense, when it uses the phrase "may also delight" and correctly translates *gaudiis in caelo* as "his gladness in heaven." There is no mention of "kingdom" in the Latin text. There is a rich metaphor found in delighting in his (Jesus') gladness in heaven that makes the previous translation ("bring us to eternal joy in the kingdom of heaven") sound rather flat and theoretical. In short, the new translation captures more adequately the true meaning and the metaphors found in the Latin text.

Lent

One of the Collects that sets the tone for Lent is the Collect for Ash Wednesday. It is short, concise, and to the point. Let's look at the actual texts of the Collect:

Previous Translation	New Translation

Lord,
protect us in our struggle
   against evil.
As we begin the *discipline*
   of Lent,
make this day *holy* by our
   self-denial.
	Grant, O Lord, that we may
	   begin with holy *fasting*
	this *campaign* of *Christian service*,
	so that, as we take up battle
	   against spiritual evils,
	we may be *armed* with *weapons*
	   of self-restraint.

In the previous translation, I italicized all of the words that do not appear in the Latin text. In the new translation, I italicized all of the words that did appear in the Latin text but are missing from the previous translation. You will notice the significant differences between these two prayers. If you translate all the words in Latin and retain the metaphors found in the Latin text, you will find a beautiful expression of our Catholic faith. In the interest of providing a modern-day equivalent to the words in the

Latin text, the previous translation frequently lost a good deal of the poetry and charm of the Roman tradition of prayer.

The previous translation asks God to "protect us in our struggle against evil," rather than making use of the powerful metaphor of being "armed with weapons of self-restraint." Perhaps there was a reluctance to introduce the metaphor of a "battle" at the beginning of Lent; yet the theme of the "battle against spiritual evils" is a very important theme during Lent.

While some translators wondered if using the metaphor "campaign of Christian service" (in Latin, *praesidia militiae christianae*) would interject political overtones into this prayer, it is clear in Latin that the principal theme of this Collect is the "battle against spiritual evils." This was also a major theme in the writings of the Fathers of the Church. Hence, the decision was made to retain this imagery of a campaign when referring to our Christian service.

The previous translation ("struggle against evil") sounds rather weak when compared to the new translation ("battle against spiritual evils"). The Latin text (*spiritualis nequitias*) clearly refers to spiritual evils. Yet the previous translation fails to mention the important adjective "spiritual." Our battle during Lent is not a material conquest, but a battle for spiritual victory over the evils that have afflicted our lives as persons and as community.

The powerful image of being "armed with weapons of self-restraint" is largely missing from the previous translation. It does refer to "self-denial," but the new translation uses a fresher, more thought-provoking way to translate the Latin word *continentiae*. In short, the new translation does a better job of preserving the overall image of a battle against spiritual evils and introduces the important themes of "fasting" and "self-restraint" as part of our reflection on this first day of Lent.

HOLY WEEK

The Collect for Palm Sunday of the Passion of the Lord is rich in beautiful metaphors and expressive language, preparing us to listen attentively to the scripture readings that follow this prayer. Let's examine the text of this Collect.

Previous Translation	New Translation
Almighty, ever-living God, you have given the human race Jesus Christ our Savior as a model of humility. He fulfilled your will by becoming man and giving his life on the cross. Help us to bear witness to you by following his example of suffering and make us worthy to share in his resurrection.	Almighty ever-living God, who as an example of humility for the human race to *follow* *caused* our Savior *to take flesh* and *submit* to the Cross, *graciously* grant that we may *heed his lesson* of *patient* suffering and so *merit a share* in his Resurrection.

The first thing you notice is the close similarity in translation of the two Collects. Apparently, when ICEL translated the prayers during Holy Week, they tended to use a more literal translation, overcoming the temptation to summarize or provide a contemporary interpretation of the Latin text. It's in the second half of the Collect that the problems start to surface.

The previous translation asks God to "make us worthy to share in his resurrection," while the new translation simply says, "and so merit a share in his Resurrection." The Latin words, "*concede propitious*," mean "graciously grant," not "help us to bear witness to you." The old translation is an interpretation that hides the real meaning of the Latin text: "graciously grant that we may heed his lesson of patient suffering." There is no reference to the adjective "patient" in the old translation.

While the Latin verb *mereamur* could be translated as "make us worthy," in its context at the end of the prayer it is clearer to translate this verb as "merit." Using "merit" helps to return to the petition earlier in the prayer where we asked God to help us "heed his lesson of patient suffering." In other words, if we unite our sufferings to those of the Lord, we can then expect to share in the glory of his Resurrection.

While the changes in the two translations may appear minor, the word selection is important. The new translation's image of a "gracious" God, of people attentive to Jesus' example of patient suffering, and of our efforts at spiritual renewal meriting a share in the Resurrection can make a difference in the overall meaning and impact of this prayer.

THE SACRED PASCHAL TRIDUUM

The Sacred Paschal Triduum begins with the Thursday of the Lord's Supper at the Evening Mass. The Collect of this Mass draws upon the rich biblical tradition associated with the Institution of the Eucharist by Jesus at the Last Supper and looks forward to his saving Death on Good Friday. Let's look at the text of this Collect.

Previous Translation	New Translation
God our Father, *we are gathered here* to share in the supper which your only Son left to his Church *to reveal his* love. He gave it to us when he was about to die and commanded us to celebrate it as the new and eternal sacrifice. We pray that *in this eucharist* we *may find* the fullness of love and life.	O God, who *have called us to participate* in this *most sacred* Supper, in which your Only *Begotten* Son, when *about to hand himself over* to death, *entrusted* to the Church a sacrifice new for all eternity, the *banquet* of his love, *grant*, we pray, that *we may draw from so great a mystery*, the fullness of charity and of life.

As we saw on Palm Sunday, during Holy Week the translation tends to be more literal, and thus we have only a few differences between the old and new translation. I italicized the words in the previous translation that are an interpretation rather than a literal translation of the Latin text. However, these are minor differences. The main difficulty is at the beginning of the prayer.

The Latin text clearly speaks of God's call at the Last Supper to participate in this most sacred banquet. Active participation in the Mass was one of the goals of the Second Vatican Council's *Constitution on the Sacred Liturgy* and of many statements from Church Fathers and Popes down through the centuries. The decision to translate *frequentantibus* in Latin as "gather" (*frequentantibus*) literally means to celebrate or to participate in a festival) unfortunately did not serve us well. It obscured the deeper meaning of the Latin text.

One of the goals of the new translation was to use the Latin word order, when possible, in order to preserve the emphasis found in the Latin text. You see this goal being implemented when the new translation puts the adjective "new" after the word "sacrifice" and changes "eternal" to "for all eternity" (*novum in saecula* in Latin). There is an emphasis here that the previous translation ("left to his Church to reveal his love") fails to fully convey.

One major improvement that the new translation makes for the Sacred Paschal Triduum is to provide an up-to-date text for parishes to use in the rites of Baptism, Confirmation, and reception into full communion with the Catholic Church for the "Easter Vigil in the Holy Night [of Easter]." Note that there is a new, more precise title for the Easter Vigil in the new translation. In the past, priests needed to use texts taken from the *Rite of Christian Initiation of Adults* (RCIA) in place of what was printed in *The Sacramentary* and most worship aids and disposable missals, which followed the text from the previous edition of *The Sacramentary*, but did not use the new texts found in the RCIA. Now both priests and people will have an easier time following the Christian Initiation Rites celebrated during the Easter Vigil.

EASTER TIME

The Collect of the Mass for Easter Sunday (At the Mass during the Day) is probably one of the most well known texts in *The Roman Missal*. Let's look at the improvements the new translation made in this well-known Collect.

Previous Translation	New Translation

God our Father,
by raising Christ your Son
you conquered the *power*
   of death
and opened for us the way
   to eternal life.
Let our *celebration* today
raise us up and renew
   our lives
by the Spirit that is
   within us.
	O God, who on this day,
	through your Only Begotten Son,
	have conquered death
	and unlocked for us the path
	   to eternity,
	grant, we pray, that we who keep
	the *solemnity of the Lord's*
	   Resurrection
	may, through the renewal *brought*
	   by your Spirit,
	rise up *in the light of life.*

The new translation follows more closely the word order in the Latin text than did the previous translation. There are two words used in the previous translation that are not found in the Latin text (see the italicized words). There are several phrases and one verb that the previous translation did not include (see the italicized words). While the previous translation is close to the Latin text, it does not completely capture the flavor of the Latin Collect.

One of the hallmarks of the Roman tradition of prayer is conciseness and directness. It is more concise to say "conquered death" than to say "conquered the power of death." The word for "power" is not found in the Latin text. The word used to describe the celebration of the Lord's Resurrection is "solemnity," from the Latin word *sollemnia*. However, the previous translation tended to avoid using the word "solemnity" in favor of the simpler word "celebration." Yet Easter Sunday ranks as a solemnity, the major celebration of the whole liturgical year. "Solemnity" conveys a sense of something special, formal, and impressive. "Celebration" misses out on some of these connotations.

The previous translation did not include the phrase "of the Lord's Resurrection." Perhaps it seemed redundant. However, *resurrectionis dominicae* is found in the Latin text. Not to translate it is to miss specifying one of the great mysteries of our faith: the Lord's Resurrection. The new translation could be improved by translating the verb *colimus* as "we who celebrate" rather than simply saying "we who keep." Perhaps the translators wanted to find another word besides "celebrate" for the sake of variety.

The reference to the Spirit bringing about our renewal in faith is clearer and more emphatic in the new translation, which adds the verb "brought" before the phrase, "by your Spirit." It is puzzling to figure out why the previous translation did not add the words "in the light of faith" to the end of the prayer. After all, this is what the Latin text says: *in lumine vitae.* "Light of faith" is a major theme and metaphor in our Catholic prayer tradition. The previous translation did not preserve this metaphor.

In short, the changes in the new translation are relatively few, but they do affect the impact of this prayer upon those who hear it. Not to mention the "Lord's Resurrection" in the Collect for Easter Sunday is to miss a major emphasis in the Latin prayer. The same thing is true of "light of faith." The new translation was careful to restore major theological themes and images contained in the Latin text. Hopefully, this new translation of this famous Collect will have an even greater impact on people than the previous translation had.

ORDINARY TIME

The *Universal Norms on the Liturgical Year and the Calendar,* 43, explains Ordinary Time in these words:

Besides the times of the year that have their own distinctive character, there remain in the yearly cycle thirty-three or thirty-four weeks in which no particular aspect of the mystery of Christ is celebrated, but rather the mystery of Christ itself is honored in its fullness, especially on Sundays. This period is known as Ordinary Time.

Consequently, Ordinary Time is meant to be the time when we unfold new aspects of the mystery of Christ—his whole life, his ministry, and his teachings, leading up to his saving Death and Resurrection.

While the *Lectionary for Mass* has a three-year cycle of readings, *The Roman Missal* only has a single set of presidential prayers (Collect, Prayer over the Offerings, Prayer after Communion) for each Sunday of Ordinary Time. In some ways this is unfortunate, since there is not always a direct connection between the Collect and the scripture readings that immediately follow. Nonetheless, I believe people will enjoy the clarity, poetry, and beauty of these prayers.

One interesting addition to this part of *The Roman Missal* is the addition of a new heading, "Sunday and Daily Masses," before the previous heading "First Week in Ordinary Time" (which was retained). The goal in adding this new heading was to specify that the prayers assigned to the Sundays of Ordinary Time could also be used during the week. Moreover, there is no good reason why a priest cannot select a different Mass from Ordinary Time than the one he celebrated on Sunday in order to provide more variety in the prayers used at daily Mass. For daily Mass, I try to look through the Masses of Ordinary Time to find a Collect that better fits the scripture readings for daily Mass than the one assigned to last Sunday. Of course, this applies to those days when there is not a Collect of a saint or a feast assigned for that day.

There are some wonderful Collects in the Masses of Ordinary Time. Let's look at the Collect from the Fifth Sunday in Ordinary Time:

Previous Translation	New Translation
Father, watch over your family and keep us safe in your care, for all our hope is *in you.*	Keep your family *safe,* O Lord, with *unfailing* care, that, *relying solely* on the *hope of* *heavenly grace,* *they may be defended always by* *your protection.*

The Collects of Ordinary Time were frequently more summaries than literal translations of the Latin text. They frequently corrected the word order of the Latin text and eliminated metaphors, modifiers, adjectives, adverbs, the superlative case, and even biblical references. The result was a prayer that tended to be bland and uninteresting. Often I have heard people say that they think the Collect is boring. This is unfortunate, since the content of these prayers is truly remarkable.

The new translation aims to restore the full depth and power of these important presidential prayers. You can see this in the example above from the Fifth Sunday of Ordinary Time. In the previous translation I italicized the words that are not found in the Latin text. In the new translation I italicized the words that were not translated in the previous text, but are found in the original Latin text. At least a third of the prayer was never fully translated. No wonder people complained that the opening Collects were bland and uninteresting. They really did not have an accurate or adequate English translation to guide their prayer.

The Latin text refers to God as "Lord," not "Father." In addition, the reference to "O Lord" is *after* the beautiful petition, "Keep your family safe." The Latin text also refers to God's "unfailing care" (*continua pietate* in Latin), which the previous translation abbreviated as simply "your care." The hope that God will not fail us is an important aspect of Christian belief. Unfortunately, the previous translation did not do justice to this theme. "Relying solely on the hope of heavenly grace" became in the previous translation the much simpler statement "for all our hope is in you." Yet, when we say we are relying solely on the hope of heavenly grace, we are again speaking of a reality that people can very much identify with. How many times have we heard the familiar saying: "There but for the grace of God go I." To fail to mention the hope given us by God's "grace" impoverishes the meaning of this prayer.

That "we may be defended always by your protection" puts into words a prayer every one of us has said to God at some point in our life. Unfortunately, the previous translation abbreviated this clause into "keep us safe in your care." The Latin text says *tua semper protectione muniatur*, and the new text provides a literal translation of the Latin. I draw comfort from hearing that I am defended by God's protection. Life in the big city (I live in Chicago) can often be rather dangerous. It's good to know that I have a heavenly protector to depend on.

Solemnities of the Lord during Ordinary Time

There are four Solemnities of the Lord that take place during Ordinary Time. In order to find them more easily, they are grouped together immediately after the Sundays of Ordinary Time. Since we have thirty-three or thirty-four Sundays in Ordinary Time, it shouldn't be too difficult to find these solemnities in our 1,500-page Roman Missal.

After completing Easter Time with the celebration of Pentecost, we have two solemnities, the Most Holy Trinity and the Most Holy Body and Blood of Christ (also known by its Latin name, *Corpus Christi*), before we begin using the texts for the numbered Sundays of Ordinary Time. These solemnities celebrate two important doctrines: the Trinity and the Eucharist.

The Solemnity of the Most Sacred Heart of Jesus is traditionally celebrated on a Friday after the Second Sunday after Pentecost. Since Easter Sunday and Pentecost are celebrated on different days each year due to the tradition of celebrating Easter on the Sunday after the first full moon of the vernal equinox, the date for the Solemnity of the Most Sacred Heart of Jesus is also variable.

The Solemnity of Our Lord Jesus Christ, King of the Universe, closes Ordinary Time. The next Sunday marks the beginning of Advent. However, it is important to remember that all these Solemnities of the Lord are grouped together in one place in *The Roman Missal*, even though they are celebrated on different days each year.

Let's look at the Collect from the Solemnity of the Most Holy Body and Blood of Christ:

Previous Translation	New Translation
Lord Jesus Christ, you gave us the eucharist as the memorial of your *suffering* and *death*. May our *worship* of *this sacrament* of your body and blood help us to experience the salvation you *won for us* and *the peace of the kingdom*. . .	O God, who in this *wonderful Sacrament* have left us a memorial of your Passion, grant us, we pray, so to *revere* the *sacred mysteries* of your Body and Blood that we may always experience in ourselves the *fruits* of your redemption.

In the previous translation I italicized all of the words that are not found in the Latin text, but really are a new composition, which changes the meaning of this prayer. In the new translation I italicized the words that the previous text failed to translate. When you translate all the words in the Latin text and follow more closely the word order of the Latin, you have a remarkably concise and beautiful prayer celebrating the wonderful sacrament that is the Holy Eucharist, the Body and Blood of Christ.

The Latin text refers to "wonderful Sacrament" (*sacramento mirabilis*). It doesn't mention the word Eucharist. The sacrament of the Eucharist is indeed a great wonder. To think that God would be present under the appearances of bread and wine is indeed a "wonderful" thing. To recognize the fact that the Eucharist is one of the seven sacraments is an important aspect of Catholic teaching. The word "Sacrament" was deliberately chosen to bring out the importance of the Eucharistic celebration, which makes present the Body and Blood of Christ.

The Latin text refers to the "memorial" of Our Lord's "Passion" (*passionis tuae memoriam*), not his "suffering and death." The previous translation sometimes resorts to explanations of what the words in the Latin text mean, rather than relying on people's ability to recognize terms used when speaking about the sacred mysteries. In fact, the Latin text does refer to sacred mysteries (*sacra mysteria*), not to the worship of this sacrament. The Latin word the previous translation translates as "worship" is really *venerari*. In English, we translate this verb as "venerate." To venerate something is to honor it, revere it, treat it with reverence and respect—important concepts that are inadequately conveyed by the word "worship." Hence, the new translation chooses the word "revere" in order to translate more accurately *venerari*.

In the second half of the Collect we are asking God to help us always to experience "the fruits" of God's redemption of the human race. The Latin text clearly refers to "fruits" (*redemptionis tuae fructum*). To simply say "to experience the salvation" fails to convey the full meaning of the Latin text. The help and inspiration we receive from God each day, especially in our reception of the Holy Body and Blood of Christ, are the fruits of our redemption. The way the old text translates the Latin shifts the emphasis to the theological concept of "salvation" rather than the impact of salvation in us, namely the "fruits of your redemption."

There is a precision that must be maintained in translating the Latin prayers. If we are not careful, we can change the emphasis of the prayer and not fully convey the depth of meaning that is found in the particular Collect we are praying. Little things like using the reference to "sacred mysteries" rather than to "this sacrament" really do have an impact overall on the effectiveness of this prayer to help us enter into the mysteries that we are celebrating. Simply put, the new translation is more accurate and effective as a prayer than the previous translation.

QUESTIONS FOR CONTINUED REFLECTION

1. What is the value of changing the title of this section of *The Roman Missal* from the "Proper of Seasons" to the "Proper of Time"?

2. What do you think of the new translations for the Collects from the different parts of the Proper of Time?

   a) Advent
   b) Christmas Time
   c) Lent
   d) Holy Week
   e) The Sacred Paschal Triduum
   f) Easter Time
   g) Ordinary Time
   h) Solemnities of the Lord during Ordinary Time

3. Did you find the new translation to be an improvement? Why or why not?

4. How important is it to accurately translate the Latin text? Do you value the restoration of metaphors, poetic language, biblical connections, superlative adjectives, variety in the references made to God, following the Latin word order, and developing a special sacral language for use in communal prayer?

5. Do you feel you will have an easy or a hard time getting used to the new translations of the Collects in the Proper of Time?

Chapter 3
The Order of Mass

The next part of *The Roman Missal* is called the Order of Mass. Order comes from the Latin word, *ordo*, which refers to the "ordinary" or usual texts used by our priests and people in the celebration of the Eucharist. Hence, the Order (*Ordo*) of Mass includes the following:

- The Sign of the Cross and the Greeting
- The Penitential Act
- The Gloria
- The people's responses
- The Creed
- The prayers and responses recited during the Preparation of the Gifts
- Four revised texts of the Eucharistic Prayer
- The prayers found in the Communion Rite, including the Lamb of God
- The texts found in the Concluding Rite

The Collect, the Prayer over the Gifts, and the Prayer after Communion are found in a different part of the Missal.

Before we analyze the various parts and prayers of the Order of Mass, we need to define what we mean by the Mass. While there is a lengthy section on the celebration of the Eucharist or the Mass in the *Catechism of the Catholic Church* (CCC, 1357–1358), let me quote two paragraphs:

> We carry out this command of the Lord by celebrating the *memorial of his sacrifice*. In so doing, *we offer to the Father* what he has himself given us: the gifts

of his creation, bread and wine which, by the power
of the Holy Spirit and by the words of Christ, have
become the body and blood of Christ. Christ is thus
really and mysteriously made *present*.

We must therefore consider the Eucharist as:

— thanksgiving and praise to the *Father*;
— the sacrificial memorial of *Christ* and his Body;
— the presence of Christ by the power of his word and
   of his *Spirit*.

A good liturgical definition of the celebration of the
Eucharist or the Mass is this: The Mass is a memorial (a remem-
bering or recounting) of our communion with God and his people won for us by Jesus' willingness to lay down his life and pour
out his blood so that all may be one (in communion) with God
and each other. The big question for all of us who participate in
the Mass is this: How much do we want to be in communion
with God and his people?

Among the most often mentioned reasons for participating in the celebration of the Eucharist are the following:

- We go on Sunday because of the Third Commandment:
  "Remember the Sabbath day, to keep it holy" (CCC, 523,
  quoting Exodus 20:8–10; cf. Deuteronomy 5:12–15).
- Sunday is the Lord's Day, the day of the Resurrection, of
  numerous appearances of Jesus to his disciples, and the
  day of Pentecost, when the Holy Spirit came upon the
  Apostles and Mary. It is the day when Jesus continues
  to appear to us, to feed us, to nourish us with Word and
  Sacrament, and to unite us in love of God and neighbor.
- We go to Mass to give thanks and praise to God.
- We go to Mass to seek forgiveness for our sins.
- We go to Mass to make intercession for our needs and
  the needs of the world.

- We go to Mass to adore God, who is deserving of our expression of love and gratitude.
- We need to hear God speak to us in scripture.
- We want to receive Holy Communion.
- We need to remind ourselves of who we are and why we are members of the Church, the body of Christ.
- We enjoy hearing about our heroes (the saints and especially Mary).
- We enjoy liturgical time (Advent, Christmas Time, Ordinary Time, Lent, the Sacred Paschal Triduum, and Easter Time).

THE INTRODUCTORY RITES

The purpose or goal of the Introductory Rites is defined in the *General Instruction of the Roman Missal*, 46:

> The rites that precede the Liturgy of the Word . . .
> have the character of a beginning, an introduction,
> and a preparation.
>
> Their purpose is to ensure that the faithful, who come
> together as one, establish communion and dispose
> themselves properly to listen to the Word of God and
> to celebrate the Eucharist worthily.

Notice key phrases like "to ensure that the faithful . . . come together as one," to "establish communion," to attain the proper disposition to "listen to the Word of God", and "to celebrate the Eucharist worthily."

Like the preface of a good book, which introduces you to the major themes and characters in the book, our Introductory Rites need to gather us as one. Hence the importance of the priest and ministers processing through the assembly in order to unite the people in prayer, to facilitate leaving behind whatever thoughts and activities they were previously engaged in, and to turn their minds and hearts to the experience of communion with God and others.

The Greeting

In the Introductory Rite, there are three greetings by the priest. Their wordings are slightly different from what we are used to. The reason they sound different is that the revised translation makes clearer the biblical text on which the greetings are based.

Using biblical greetings reminds us of the 2,000 years of tradition upon which our faith is based. People have been gathering since the earliest days of the Church to celebrate the Eucharist with their priest or Bishop. There is a communion of saints praying with us both in heaven and on earth.

The three greetings by the priest are the following:

- "The grace of our Lord Jesus Christ, / and the love of God, / and the communion (rather than "fellowship") of the Holy Spirit / be with you all." It is a direct quote from 2 Corinthians 13:13.
- "Grace to you and peace from God our Father / and the Lord Jesus Christ." See Romans 1:7: "To all God's beloved in Rome, who are called to be saints: Grace to you and peace from God our Father and the Lord Jesus Christ." See also 1 Corinthians 1:3; 2 Corinthians 1:2; Galatians 1:3; Ephesians 1:2; Philippians 1:2; 1 Thessalonians 1:1; Philemon 3; Colossians 1:2; 2 Thessalonians 1:2; 1 Peter 1:3; Revelation 1:4; 1 Timothy 1:2; Titus 1:4; and 2 John 3. Obviously, the biblical wording of this greeting is quite common in the New Testament, and now the parallel with scripture has been restored.
- "The Lord be with you." See Ruth 2:4. No change is needed here.
- The response to the greeting of the priest has been retranslated more literally from the Latin: "And with your spirit." (See Galatians 6:18: "May the grace of our Lord Jesus Christ be with your spirit, brothers and sisters.")

"And with your spirit" is probably the most surprising change. Yet, if you look at the translation of *The Roman Missal* in other languages (for example, French, German, Italian, Polish, Portuguese, and Spanish), you will find that these other language groups retained the response, "And with your spirit." It was ICEL and the English-speaking countries that used a more general translation. Going back to "And with your spirit" restores a greater sense of unity with the prayer tradition of the Church used in *The Roman Missal* and in other language groups.

The response, "And with your spirit," makes clear the biblical connection between our prayer texts and scripture. In addition to Galatians 6:18 quoted above, there is also 2 Timothy 4:22: "The Lord be with your spirit." For Saint Paul, the spirit (in Greek, *pneuma*) is "the spiritual part of man that is closest to God, the immediate object of divine influence, and in particular the receptacle of the Spirit of God."

It is also important to remember that the response "And with your spirit" is said to the Priest Celebrant of the Eucharist. The assembly is recognizing the ordination of the priest who is guided by the Spirit in leading the community in prayer. The "spirit" in "And with your spirit" is the spirit the priest received in ordination that empowers him to act as another Christ in ministering to his people.

A more literal translation of *Et cum spiritu tuo* was called for in *Liturgiam authenticam*, issued by the Vatican on March 28, 2001. The desire was to restore both the biblical connections that were lost by using "And also with you" as well as to bring the English translation into oneness with the vast majority of language groups that retained "And with your spirit."

In the greeting, "The grace of our Lord Jesus Christ, / and the love of God, / and the communion of the Holy Spirit / be with you all," people will undoubtedly notice the change of wording from "fellowship of the Holy Spirit" to "communion of the Holy Spirit." In 2 Corinthians 13:13 Paul uses the Greek word *koinōnia*, which is translated as *communicatio* in the Vulgate translation of the New Testament. The usual modern translation of the Greek word *koinōnia* and the Latin word *communicatio* is "communion."

Introductory Statements

After the greeting, rubric number 3 says, as it did previously, "the priest, or a Deacon or another minister, may very briefly introduce the faithful to the Mass of the day." There has been no change to this rubric.

Rite for the Blessing and Sprinkling of Water

In the previous translation, the Rite of Blessing and Sprinkling Holy Water immediately followed the opening greeting and repeated these same texts in Appendix I of the previous edition of *The Sacramentary*. Rather than duplicate texts, the new Missal has the Rite for the Blessing and Sprinkling of Water (note the slight change in the title, "Rite for the Blessing" rather than "Rite of Blessing" and "Water" rather than "Holy Water") in the Appendix of the third edition of *The Roman Missal*. Since we use the Penitential Act rather than the Sprinkling Rite most of the time, this should not pose a problem. The Rite for the Blessing and Sprinkling of Water is still in the book, but the priest now has to mark the place at the end of the book where the blessing is found (in most new editions of the Missal, this can be marked with one of the ribbons).

Penitential Act

There is only one option (not three, as in the previous translation) for the priest's introduction to the Penitential Act: "Brethren (brothers and sisters), let us acknowledge our sins, / and so prepare ourselves to celebrate the sacred mysteries." The main change here is in the choice of verb: "let us acknowledge" rather than the old "call to mind our sins." The Latin word *agnoscamus* indicates not only an internal act of "calling to mind" but also an external act of confession, which is what is supposed to happen at this point.

There is no mention of using "similar words" of our own creation in place of this introduction to the Penitential Act. And so, if the priest wants to do a personal introduction to the Mass of the day, he should end his introduction by using the approved introduction to the Penitential Act found in the new translation. By using a common introduction, we facilitate people moving into penitential mode, in which they recognize their sinfulness and need of God's forgiveness.

As people who desire a deeper communion with God and others, we recognize that sin hinders our growth in the spiritual life. We also remember the famous words of Jesus who, in Matthew 5:23–24, says: "if you remember that your brother or sister has something against you, leave your gift there before the altar and go; first be reconciled to your brother or sister, and then come and offer your gift." Therefore, it is appropriate at the very beginning of Mass to recall our needs for reconciliation and forgiveness before moving more deeply into the sacred mysteries.

The *Confiteor* during the Penitential Act restores the gesture of striking the breast while saying "through my fault, through my fault, / through my most grievous fault." The previous translation has us striking the breast once. I suspect many people stopped doing this, and so reintroducing it may take some time. However, striking the breast does impress upon us the reality of our sinfulness and our need for reconciliation and forgiveness.

The problem we face in English-speaking countries is that the *Confiteor* that was found in the Latin version of *The Roman Missal* was edited by ICEL in the previous translation. Other language groups retained a translation more faithful to the Latin text. These language groups will only have minor changes in the wording of the *Confiteor*. If you liked the translation of the Penitential Act in the old Saint Joseph Missal from the days of the Latin Mass, you will be quite comfortable with the new ICEL translation.

Let's look at the differences in the two texts:

Previous Translation Option I	New Translation Option I
I confess to almighty God, and to you, my brothers and sisters, that I have sinned through my own fault *They strike their breast:* in my thoughts and in my words, in what I have done, and in what I have failed to do; and I ask blessed Mary, ever virgin, all the angels and saints, and you, my brothers and sisters, to pray for me to the Lord our God.	I confess to almighty God and to you, my brothers and sisters, that I have greatly sinned, in my thoughts and in my words, in what I have done and in what I have failed to do, *And, striking their breast, they say:* through my fault, through my fault, through my most grievous fault; *Then they continue:* therefore I ask blessed Mary ever-Virgin, all the Angels and Saints, and you, my brothers and sisters, to pray for me to the Lord our God.

Striking the breast or the heart reminds us of the "heart-felt" contrition for sin that we should strive for during the Penitential Act. It also restores the connection with the famous biblical story of the Pharisee and the tax collector: Luke 18:9–14, where the tax collector prayed in the back of the temple, not even daring to raise his eyes to heaven. All he did was beat his breast and say: "'God, be merciful to me, a sinner!' I tell you, this man went down to his home justified rather than the other."

The priest's prayer of absolution to the Penitential Act has not changed but retains the familiar wording of this concluding prayer:

Concluding Prayer
May almighty God have mercy on us,   forgive us our sins,   and bring us to everlasting life.

Note that this prayer asking God's forgiveness of our sins is referred to as *absolution*: "The absolution by the Priest follows." The first meaning of the word *absolutio* in Latin is "forgiveness." People may hear the word "absolution" and think that this is sacramental absolution like that which we receive in the Sacrament of Penance. This is not the case.

This concluding prayer is meant to sum up the thoughts and desires of all those who are praying for God's forgiveness. Notice that the fact that the priest says "have mercy on *us*, / forgive *us* . . . / bring *us* . . . ." The priest includes himself in the prayer. He is not acting *in persona Christi* by sacramentally absolving us for there is no mention of the formula: "I absolve you of your sins in the name of the Father, and of the Son, and of the Holy Spirit."

Option II of the Penitential Act also has changed in its wording:

Previous Translation Option II	New Translation Option II
Lord, we have sinned against you: Lord, have mercy. R. Lord, have mercy.	Have mercy on us, O Lord. R. For we have sinned against you.

Lord, show us your mercy
     and love.
 R. And grant us your salvation.
	Show us, O Lord, your mercy.
	 R. And grant us your
	     salvation.

The previous text repeated the word "Lord" more often than it was found in the Latin text. It also added the words "and love" which were not found in the Latin text. The new translation is more faithful to the wording and word order of the Latin text.

Option III of the Penitential Act provides a sample text that retains the previous wording with only a slight change in the third petition: "You are seated at the right hand of the Father *to intercede for us*: Lord, have mercy." The previous text read: "You plead for us at the right hand of the Father: Lord, have mercy." The new translation more accurately retains the meaning of the Latin text and strengthens its biblical connection.

The previous edition of *The Sacramentary* included eight petitions for Penitential Act, option III. These are not found in the new edition of *The Roman Missal*; however, other petitions for option III may also be used (see rubric number 6). Using other petitions does not exclude Priest Celebrants from using those found in the previous edition of *The Sacramentary*. Rubric number 6 states: "The priest, or a Deacon or another minister, then says the following or other invocations with Kyrie eleison (Lord, have mercy)." In the footnote on this page in the Missal we are reminded that "sample invocations are found in Appendix VI, pp. 1474–1480."

The Kyrie

The Kyrie follows (if this text was not already used in the Penitential Act). No changes have been made to this text.

The Gloria

We are reminded that we have gathered to give praise and thanks to God in the beautiful Gloria, which is modeled on the song of the angels at the birth of Christ found in Luke 2:13–14: "And suddenly there was with the angel a multitude of the heavenly host, praising God and saying: 'Glory to God in the highest heaven, / and on earth peace among those whom he favors!'" And so we unite with the angels in heaven who have the privilege of experiencing the glory of God in his heavenly kingdom, a privilege we also hope to gain.

The first line of the Gloria is slightly changed to follow exactly the wording of the Latin text: "Glory to God in the highest, / and on earth peace to people of good will." This change brings us into accord with other language groups that followed a more literal translation of the Latin text. Let's look at the two texts:

Previous Translation	New Translation
Glory to God in the highest, and peace to his people on earth.	Glory to God in the highest, and on earth peace to people of good will.
Lord God, heavenly King, almighty God and Father, we worship you, we give you thanks, we praise you for your glory.	We praise you, we bless you, we adore you, we glorify you, we give you thanks for your great glory, Lord God, heavenly King, O God, almighty Father.
Lord Jesus Christ, only Son of the Father, Lord God, Lamb of God, you take away the sin of the world: have mercy on us; you are seated at the right hand of the Father: receive our prayer.	Lord Jesus Christ, Only Begotten Son, Lord God, Lamb of God, Son of the Father, you take away the sins of the world, have mercy on us; you take away the sins of the world, receive our prayer; you are seated at the right hand of the Father, have mercy on us.
For you alone are the Holy One, you alone are the Lord, you alone are the Most High, Jesus Christ, with the Holy Spirit, in the glory of God the Father. Amen.	For you alone are the Holy One, you alone are the Lord, you alone are the Most High, Jesus Christ, with the Holy Spirit, in the glory of God the Father. Amen.

As you can see, there are also some minor revisions in the text, usually a change in the English word order to follow the logic of the Latin text:

- The first change in the word order that people will notice follows the first line quoted above. In the previous text, we went from "peace to his people on earth" to "Lord God, heavenly King, / almighty God and Father." However, this was not the word order found in the Latin text. The new translation follows the Latin word order. We move from "Glory to God in the highest, / and on earth peace to people of good will" to "We praise you, / we bless you, / we adore you, / we glorify you, / we give you thanks for your great glory, / Lord God, heavenly King, O God, almighty Father."

- The new translation also restores the full listing of the titles of Jesus exactly as they appear in the Latin text: "Lord Jesus Christ, / Only Begotten Son, / Lord God, Lamb of God, Son of the Father." The previous translation failed to translate the adjective "Only Begotten" (or *unigenite*).

- The new translation corrects an error in the previous text which failed to translate the plural noun, *peccata*, as "sins." And so we now have: "you take away the *sins* of the world" (emphasis added).

In short, we now have a Gloria whose text is in accord with its Latin source and reflects the translation found in most major languages throughout the world.

Collect

The new translation of the Collects (formerly called the Opening Prayer) eliminates the alternative prayers for Sunday Masses, which many people found to be too long, too preachy, and not in keeping with the Roman tradition. One improvement that will be immediately noticeable in the Collects is a greater sensitivity to the themes found in the scriptures for Sunday Mass. However, the wording of some of the Collects will sound strange, at least initially. The priest will have to read the prayers before Mass in order to sound comfortable praying them at Mass.

Rather than say "Opening Prayer," we now call this prayer the "Collect." "Collect" is an ancient and venerable title that hints at the purpose of this prayer: to collect our thoughts into one and to prepare us to hear the Word of God in the readings from scripture. Various Collects will be analyzed throughout this book. For specific examples, refer to Chapter Two (Proper of Time) and take a second look at the Collect for the First Sunday of Advent and the Mass during the Night at Christmas.

QUESTIONS FOR CONTINUED REFLECTION

1. What do we mean by the Order of Mass?

2. What is the Mass, and why do you go to Mass?

3. What is the purpose of the Introductory Rite?

4. Do you favor using biblical quotes to greet people at Mass?

5. Do you understand the rationale for changing the response from "and also with you" to "and with your spirit"?

6. What is the rationale behind having a Penitential Act at the beginning of Mass? Is this a time when you personally ask God to forgive your sins? Do you like returning to the practice of striking the breast?

7. Does the new wording of the Gloria appeal to you? Do you see value in using a more literal translation that corresponds more closely to the Latin text as did most other major languages in their translation?

8. Will the changes in wording in the Collect bring out a greater sense of the sacred as well as restoring images or metaphors lost in the previous translation?

Liturgy of the Word

The *General Instruction of the Roman Missal* (GIRM), 55, articulates the purpose of the Liturgy of the Word:

> The main part of the Liturgy of the Word is made up of the readings from Sacred Scripture together with the chants occurring between them. As for the Homily, the Profession of Faith, and the Universal Prayer, they develop and conclude it. For in the readings, as explained by the Homily, God speaks to his people, opening up to them the mystery of redemption and salvation, and offering spiritual nourishment; and Christ himself is present through his word in the midst of the faithful.
>
> By silence and by singing, the people make this divine word their own, and affirm their adherence to it by means of the Profession of Faith; finally, having been nourished by the divine word, the people pour out their petitions by means of the Universal Prayer for the needs of the whole Church and for the salvation of the whole world.

These are noble goals. Do we see the Liturgy of the Word opening up the mystery of redemption and salvation for us?

GIRM, 57, says: "In the readings, the table of God's Word is spread before the faithful, and the treasures of the Bible are opened to them." Do we see ourselves feasting at the table of the Word, where God nourishes our faith and instills in us the desire to live by his holy Word? Do we see the value in proclaiming readings from the Old Testament, the Epistles of the

New Testament, and the four accounts of the Gospel? Why do we use readings from the Bible rather than readings from a Pope, a council, a famous theologian, a saint, etc.?

The Bible is the one book against which all Christians at all times in all places have measured their growth in the Christian life. We believe that the Bible is inspired by God and that when the Bible is proclaimed, God himself is speaking to us in the scriptures, bringing us to conversion. No other book can claim this same divine inspiration and effectiveness in nourishing the faith of God's people.

The rubrics in the new translation of *The Roman Missal* make no reference to the priest giving an introduction to the scripture readings. While this may have been helpful when the new Missal and *Lectionary for Mass* were first introduced in 1970, it is usually not necessary today. However, a brief reference in the parish bulletin to the readings of scripture for next Sunday may be a good way to assist those who like to prepare ahead of time for Sunday Mass.

Regarding the Responsorial Psalm, rubric number 11 simply states: "The psalmist or cantor sings or says the Psalm, with the people making the response." Psalms are songs meant to be sung. Singing the Psalm is the normal way for the people to make their response to the first reading. Reading the Psalm is really the exception to the rule, at least as far as Sunday Mass is concerned.

GIRM, 61, reminds us that the Responsorial Psalm after the First Reading

> is an integral part of the Liturgy of the Word and ... has great liturgical and pastoral importance, since it fosters meditation on the Word of God. ... The Responsorial Psalm should correspond to each reading and should usually be taken from the Lectionary. ... It is preferable for the Responsorial Psalm to be sung, at least as far as the people's response is concerned.

Remember the old saying: "to sing once is to pray twice." It takes more concentrated effort to sing. Singing provides a beauty and an impact that a recited Responsorial Psalm does not have.

Deacon's Request for a Blessing

There is a more colloquial way in which the deacon asks the priest for a blessing prior to proclaiming the Gospel. The deacon will now say: "Your blessing, Father." This is a short form of the request: "*Please give me* your blessing, Father" (emphasis added). The deacon used to say: "Father, give me your blessing." The previous form always sounded a bit artificial—we usually don't begin our requests by saying "pray."

Priest's Prayer for the Deacon

There is only a minor change to the prayer of the priest for the deacon.

Previous Translation	New Translation
The Lord be in your heart and on your lips that you may worthily proclaim his gospel. In the name of the Father, and of the Son, ✚ and of the Holy Spirit.	May the Lord be in your heart and on your lips, that you may proclaim his Gospel worthily and well, in the name of the Father, and of the Son, ✚ and of the Holy Spirit.

The new translation restores the use of the subjunctive (may) and translates the two adverbs (worthily *and well*), whereas the previous translation only translated one of the adverbs from the Latin text (*digne et competenter*).

The priest's prayer before proclaiming the Gospel is the same, except that the reference to "Almighty God" is moved from the beginning of the prayer to the place where it is found in the Latin text. It reads: "Cleanse my heart and my lips, almighty God, / that I may worthily proclaim your holy Gospel."

Signing the *Book of the Gospels*, the forehead, the mouth, and the breast

After the introduction to the Gospel ("A reading from the holy Gospel according to N."), the new translation retains the rubric (number 15): "and, at the same time, he makes the Sign of the Cross on the book and on his forehead, lips, and breast." Unfortunately, this gesture is sometimes forgotten by priests and deacons. Yet the use of nonverbal signs certainly appeals to people's imaginations and helps to make the proclamation of the Gospel stand out and appear truly special, a privileged moment in which Jesus speaks to his people, feeding them with his word.

Whenever I sign the book, my forehead, my lips, and my heart, I ask Jesus to truly speak his words effectively through me. It is a very powerful symbolic act whereby I open my whole being to proclaiming God's holy Word. People copy this gesture because they too want their whole being to be open to receiving God's Word, to embrace it heart and soul, to let it soak into their thoughts, words, and deeds.

Using the *Book of the Gospels* in Procession

I also want to encourage parishes to purchase a *Book of the Gospels* and use it in the procession to the ambo for the proclamation of the Gospel. Using this special book for the proclamation of the Gospel helps to remind us of the presence of Christ, who continues to teach his people when his Gospel is proclaimed. In the Gospel, it is Jesus speaking to us. This is why GIRM, 60 says:

> The reading of the Gospel constitutes the high point
> of the Liturgy of the Word. The Liturgy itself teaches
> the great reverence that is to be shown to this reading

by setting it off from the other readings with special marks of honor, by the fact of which minister is
appointed to proclaim it and by the blessing or prayer
with which he prepares himself; and also by the fact
that through their acclamations the faithful acknowledge and confess that Christ is present and is speaking
to them and stand as they listen to the reading; and by
the mere fact of the marks of reverence that are given
to the *Book of the Gospels*.

At the end of the proclamation of the Gospel, the priest
or deacon says "The Gospel of the Lord" and, according to
rubric number 16, is to kiss the *Book of the Gospels*. Again, this
nonverbal gesture is one of affection and reverence for the proclamation of the Gospel and the holy book in which Jesus' words
are found. Sometimes, the priest's or deacon's concentration on
giving the homily leads them to skip over this gesture.

Priest's Prayer after Kissing the Book

There is a prayer that priests are supposed to say when they kiss the
Book of the Gospels: "Through the words of the Gospel / may our
sins be wiped away." This prayer helps us to remember that in the
proclamation of the Gospel, we are releasing the power of Jesus to
bring us to conversion and save us from our sins. This prayer is an
important reminder of the importance of proclaiming the Gospel
in the priest's life and in the lives of God's people.

Homily

A homily is an explanation of the Word of God in the context of
daily life in order to elicit a desire for communion with God and
his people. GIRM, 65 explains it this way:

> The Homily is part of the Liturgy and is highly rec-
> ommended, for it is necessary for the nurturing of the
> Christian life. It should be an explanation of some
> aspect of the readings from Sacred Scripture or of

another text from the Ordinary or the Proper of the Mass of the day and should take into account both the mystery being celebrated and the particular needs of the listeners.

Rubric number 17 in *The Roman Missal* reminds us that the homily is an expected and necessary part of the Sunday Eucharist. It says: "Then follows the Homily, which is to be preached by a Priest or Deacon on all Sundays and Holydays of Obligation."

The Profession of Faith

The most notable change in the Liturgy of the Word that people will notice concerns the wording of the Nicene Creed. We have returned to a more accurate translation of various phrases in the Creed. *Credo*, for example, is now translated "I believe," not "We believe." In fact, the translation includes the phrase, "I believe," four times: "I believe in God," "I believe in one Lord Jesus Christ," "I believe in the Holy Spirit," and "I believe in one, holy, catholic, and apostolic Church."

The sense of renewing one's commitment in faith becomes even stronger when you realize the affective element in the words "I believe." *Credo* in Latin comes from two Latin words: *cor*, meaning "heart," and *do*, meaning "I give." To say I believe ("I give you my heart") is to tell God that you are willing to give him your heart, your whole being in living a life of faith. This is a powerful expression of love and commitment. It is similar to the love and commitment expressed by Mary in the Magnificat: "My soul magnifies the Lord, / and my spirit rejoices in God my Savior" (Luke 1:46).

This change to "I believe" reflects the liturgical tradition of each individual personally recommitting themselves to a life of faith by saying "I believe." This liturgical version of an individual assent to the words of the Creed is most obvious at the renewal of baptismal promises at the Easter Vigil and on Easter Sunday when we answer "I do."

The liturgical tradition is different from the theological tradition based on the Creed approved at the Council of Nicea, where they said "we believe." In the context of defining the core doctrines of our faith, the Bishops wanted to explain what we as Catholics believe to be true and revealed by God. This was not a liturgical context for the expression of personal faith. GIRM, 67 explains the purpose of the Creed:

> The purpose of the Creed or Profession of Faith is that the whole gathered people may respond to the Word of God proclaimed in the readings taken from Sacred Scripture and explained in the Homily and that they may also honor and confess the great mysteries of the faith by pronouncing the rule of faith in a formula approved for liturgical use and before the celebration of these mysteries in the Eucharist begins.

If the priest has his opportunity to respond to God's Word and proclaim his faith in the homily, then the Profession of Faith is the opportunity for the whole community to respond to God's Word and to proclaim their love and commitment in a very personal way.

Let me list all the places that have changed in the Creed:

- "I believe in one God." Previous translation: "We believe."
- "Of all things visible and invisible" rather than "of all that is seen and unseen." See Colossians 1:16: "for in him all things in heaven and on earth were created, things visible and invisible." ICEL has noted: "The change from the current version 'seen and unseen' was made because something can be unseen and yet in principle visible (for example, a remote galaxy) or unseen and entirely invisible (for example, an angel)."
- "The Only Begotten Son of God" rather than "the only Son of God." A more literal translation than the previous text.

- "Born of the Father before all ages" rather than "eternally begotten of the Father." A more literal translation than before.
- "Consubstantial" rather than "one in Being with the Father." Use of the correct theological term to describe the relationship between the Father and the Son was considered a better way to convey this sacred mystery.
- "And by the power of the Holy Spirit was incarnate of the Virgin Mary" rather than "by the power of the Holy Spirit / he was born of the Virgin Mary." The Bishops voted to reintroduce the theological term "incarnate" as a more precise way of describing both the moment of conception of Jesus in Mary and the moment of his birth at Bethlehem.
- "And rose again on the third day" rather than "on the third day he rose again." The new translation follows the wording of the Latin text.
- "In accordance with the Scriptures" rather than "in fulfillment of the Scriptures." A more literal translation.
- "His kingdom will have no end" rather than "*and* his kingdom will have no end" (emphasis added).
- "I believe in the Holy Spirit." Previous translation: "We believe."
- "Who with the Father and the Son is adored and glorified" rather than "with the Father and the Son is worshiped and glorified." A more literal translation of the Latin text.
- "Who has spoken through the prophets" rather than "He has spoken through the Prophets."
- "I believe in one, holy, catholic, and apostolic Church." Previous translation: "We believe."
- "I confess one Baptism for the forgiveness of sins" rather than "We acknowledge one Baptism for the forgiveness of sins." Personally "confessing one's faith" is a richer description of what is intended than the more intellectual phrase "we acknowledge one Baptism."

- "I look forward to the resurrection of the dead" rather than "We look for the resurrection of the dead."

The new translation of the Nicene Creed is as follows:

New Translation

I believe in one God,
the Father almighty,
maker of heaven and earth,
of all things visible and invisible.

I believe in one Lord Jesus Christ,
the Only Begotten Son of God,
born of the Father before all ages.
God from God, Light from Light,
true God from true God,
begotten, not made, consubstantial with the Father;
through him all things were made.
For us men and for our salvation
he came down from heaven,

At the following words, up to and including and became man, *all bow.*

and by the Holy Spirit was incarnate of the Virgin Mary,
and became man.

For our sake he was crucified under Pontius Pilate,
he suffered death and was buried,
and rose again on the third day
in accordance with the Scriptures.
He ascended into heaven
and is seated at the right hand of the Father.
He will come again in glory
to judge the living and the dead
and his kingdom will have no end.

I believe in the Holy Spirit, the Lord, the giver of life,
who proceeds from the Father and the Son,
who with the Father and the Son is adored and glorified,
who has spoken through the prophets.

I believe in one, holy, catholic, and apostolic Church.
I confess one Baptism for the forgiveness of sins
and I look forward to the resurrection of the dead
and the life of the world to come. Amen.

The three changes that stand out are "I believe" instead of "We believe"; the use of "consubstantial with the Father" instead of "one in being with the Father"; and "incarnate of the Virgin Mary" rather than "was born of the Virgin Mary."

There is great wisdom in these changes. Most other language groups retained the singular form of the verb *Credo* or "I believe." We are simply being more accurate and restoring our unity with other language groups in emphasizing the personal nature of our commitment in faith by saying "I believe," very similar to what we do at the Easter Vigil or on Easter Sunday.

Other language groups have also long maintained that "consubstantial" is the proper theological term to describe the mystery of the relationship between the Father and the Son. We are dealing with the realm of mystery, where colloquial phrases (like "one in being") diminish or fail to adequately convey the full nature of the mystery being described.

"Incarnate" is another verb meaning "born" and the correct doctrinal term to describe the mystery of Christ's conception in Mary and his birth in Bethlehem; accepting this new term should not be very difficult. The Creed proclaims the sacred mysteries. The proper term to describe the sacred mystery of Christ's conception in Mary and his birth in Bethlehem is "incarnation."

When you read the words of the Nicene Creed with its new phrases, you will find it to be easier to read than the previous version. In fact, it improves on the previous translation in certain spots. For example, "I look forward to the resurrection of the dead" more adequately expresses the hope and longing of people of faith for eternal life than the old translation ("we look for the resurrection of the dead."). The verb in Latin is *exspecto*.

Use of the Apostles' Creed in place of the Nicene Creed will continue to be an option, especially during Lent and Easter Time, according to rubric, number 19: " Instead of the Niceno-Constantinopolitan Creed, especially during Lent and Easter Time, the baptismal Symbol of the Roman Church, known as the Apostles' Creed, may be used.

The changes in the Apostles' Creed are mostly in grammar, restoring the "who" clauses found in the Latin text:

- "*And* in Jesus Christ, his only Son, our Lord," rather than "*I believe* in Jesus Christ, his only Son, our Lord."
- "*Who* was conceived by the power of the Holy Spirit" rather than "*He* was conceived by the power of the Holy Spirit."
- "Born of the Virgin Mary" rather than "*and* born of the Virgin Mary."
- "Suffered under Pontius Pilate" rather than "*He* suffered under Pontius Pilate."
- "On the third day he rose again *from the dead*" rather than "On the third day he rose again."
- "And is seated at the right hand of *God* the Father *almighty*" rather than "and is seated at the right hand of the Father."
- "*From there* he will come to judge the living and the dead" rather than "He will come again to judge the living and the dead."

There is a stronger sense of clarity of what is being affirmed in the new wording of the Apostles' Creed.

Let's look at the new translation of the Apostles' Creed:

New Translation

I believe in God,
the Father almighty,
Creator of heaven and earth,
and in Jesus Christ, his only Son, our Lord,

At the words that follow, up to and including the Virgin Mary, *all bow.*

who was conceived by the Holy Spirit,
born of the Virgin Mary,
suffered under Pontius Pilate,
was crucified, died and was buried;
he descended into hell;
on the third day he rose again from the dead;
he ascended into heaven,
and is seated at the right hand of God the Father almighty;
from there he will come to judge the living and the dead.

I believe in the Holy Spirit,
the holy catholic Church,
the communion of saints,
the forgiveness of sins,
the resurrection of the body,
and life everlasting. Amen.

The new translation of the Apostles' Creed does a better job of translating accurately the Latin text. It returns to the use of "who" clauses that are found in the Latin. Yet it is very close in wording to the old translation and retains, where possible, the word order of the previous translation. The new translation will be accepted quite easily.

The Universal Prayer or Prayer of the Faithful

The first thing you will notice is that the name is now "The Universal Prayer" rather than the "General Intercessions" that we found in the previous translation. In addition, the new translation retains the title of "Prayer of the Faithful." "Universal" rather than "general" provides a more specific description of the intent of these prayers. What is the purpose of these prayers? According to GIRM, 69:

> In the Universal Prayer or Prayer of the Faithful, the people respond in some sense to the Word of God which they have received in faith and, exercising the office of their baptismal Priesthood, offer prayers to God for the salvation of all. It is desirable that there usually be such a form of prayer in Masses celebrated with the people, so that petitions may be offered for holy Church, for those who govern with authority over us, for those weighed down by various needs, for all humanity, and for the salvation of the whole world.

GIRM, 70 further explains that the usual series of intentions is for the needs of the Church, for public authorities and the salvation of the whole world, for those burdened by any kind of difficulty, and for the local community: "Nevertheless, in any particular celebration, such as a Confirmation, a Marriage, or at a Funeral, the series of intentions may be concerned more closely with the particular occasion." While you do not want to give the impression that the total focus of attention is on local needs, there are times when the local needs require more than one petition.

GIRM, 71 gives us good advice about how to compose a petition for the Universal Prayer or Prayer of the Faithful: "The intentions announced should be sober, be composed with a wise liberty and in few words, and they should be expressive of the prayer of the entire community." Quite often, after specifying the intention, we end with the words "let us pray to the Lord." The people then know to make their response, which often is: "Lord, hear our prayer."

QUESTIONS FOR CONTINUED REFLECTION

1. What is the purpose of the Liturgy of the Word?

2. Why do we read from the Bible instead of the writings of a Pope or contemporary theologian?

3. Why is it important to sing the Responsorial Psalm?

4. What meaning do you attach to the signing with the cross of the *Book of the Gospels,* the forehead, the lips, and the breast (or heart)?

5. Why should we use a special book for proclaiming the Gospel, different from the one used for proclaiming the other scripture readings?

6. What is a genuine homily? Why are homilies restricted only to priests or deacons?

7. Why are lay people restricted to giving reflections?

8. Why the change from "We believe" to "I believe" in the Creed? Is this an improvement?

9. How would you explain the meaning of the words "consubstantial" and "incarnate" in the Creed?

10. When does your parish use the Apostles' Creed? When does GIRM recommend the option of using the Apostles' Creed?

11. What is the significance of referring to the "Universal Prayer" or "Prayer of the Faithful" in the new translation rather than continue to use the "General Intercessions," as in the previous translation?

LITURGY OF THE EUCHARIST

The Preparation of the Gifts

GIRM, 72 explains the purpose of the Preparation of the Gifts as bringing the necessary elements (bread, wine, water) to the altar: "At the Preparation of the Gifts, bread and wine with water are brought to the altar, the same elements, that is to say, which Christ took into his hands." GIRM, 73 then goes on to say: "First of all, the altar or Lord's table, which is the center of the whole Liturgy of the Eucharist, is made ready when on it are placed the corporal, purificator, Missal, and chalice (unless this last is prepared at the credence table)."

Offertory Chant

Rubric number 21 in the Order of Mass also reminds us that after the Prayer of the Faithful is completed, "the Offertory Chant begins." Once again, the preference is for singing at Sunday Mass, rather than merely reciting the two prayers of blessing. GIRM, 74 further explains: "The procession bringing the gifts is accompanied by the Offertory Chant . . . which continues at least until the gifts have been placed on the altar. The norms on the manner of singing are the same as for the Entrance Chant."

Offertory Procession

Rubric number 22 affirms the importance of the faithful "making an offering, bringing forward bread and wine for the celebration of the Eucharist and perhaps other gifts to relieve the needs of the Church and of the poor." In other words, an offertory procession with the gifts of bread and wine and other appropriate gifts, such as food for the poor, is expected to take place. While the bread and wine belong on the altar, other gifts such as money or food "are to be put in a suitable place away from the Eucharistic table" (GIRM, 73). Bringing up the gifts from a side table directly to the altar without involving the people is not an option.

Since the people are expected to be singing at this point, rubric number 23 says that the priest "takes the paten with the bread and holds it slightly raised above the altar with both hands, saying in a low voice" the prayer of blessing. Simply put, if the people are singing during the Preparation of the Gifts, the priest should not be simultaneously proclaiming in a loud voice the two prayers of blessing over the bread and the wine.

In the Preparation of the Gifts, the two "blessed are you" prayers over the bread and the wine have been re-translated slightly:

Previous Translation	New Translation
Blessed are you, Lord, God of all creation. Through your goodness we have this bread to offer, which earth has given and human hands have made. It will become for us the bread of life.	Blessed are you, Lord God of all creation, for through your goodness we have received the bread we offer you: fruit of the earth and work of human hands, it will become for us the bread of life.

The new translation is more precise in translating the Latin text than the previous translation. You see this in evidence in the reference to the "fruit of the earth and work of human hands" rather than the previous translation: "which earth has given and human hands have made." Despite the new words used, the meaning of the prayer remains the same.

The prayer over the chalice filled with wine is very close to the new text for the prayer over the bread. Consequently, it should be received fairly easily by the people. The reference to "our spiritual drink" has at its root a biblical connection, in 1 Corinthians 10:4: "and all drank the same spiritual drink." This passage from Saint Paul makes it clear that there is only one spiritual drink, namely, Christ.

Previous Translation	New Translation
Blessed are you, Lord, God of all creation. Through your goodness we have this wine to offer, fruit of the vine and work of human hands. It will become our spiritual drink.	Blessed are you, Lord God of all creation, for through your goodness we have received the wine we offer you: fruit of the vine and work of human hands, it will become our spiritual drink.

Priest's Silent Prayer

There is a slight change in the wording of the priest's prayer which he says quietly after the prayer of blessing over the chalice filled with wine. Rubric number 26 notes that the priest says this prayer while bowing profoundly.

Previous Translation	New Translation
Lord God, we ask you to receive us and be pleased with the sacrifice we offer you with humble and contrite hearts.	With humble spirit and contrite heart may we be accepted by you, O Lord, and may our sacrifice in your sight this day be pleasing to you, Lord God.

The new translation follows the Latin word order, translating all the words in the Latin text into English, something the old translation failed to do. It may take our priests some time to get used to this new translation. Since the priest says this particular prayer silently, this change should not affect our people.

This prayer is based on Daniel 3:39–40: "Yet with a contrite heart and a humble spirit may we be accepted."

Use of Incense

Rubric number 27 notes the following: "If appropriate, he [the priest] also incenses the offerings, the cross, and the altar. A

Deacon or other minister then incenses the Priest and the people." GIRM, 75 explains the significance of this incensing of the offerings, the cross, and the altar: "so as to signify the Church's offering and prayer rising like incense in the sight of God. Next, the Priest, because of his sacred ministry, and the people, by reason of their baptismal dignity, may be incensed by the Deacon or by another minister."

Prayer for Washing Hands

There is a slight change in the word order of the prayer said when washing the priest's hands: "Wash me, O Lord, from my iniquity / and cleanse me from my sin" rather than "Lord, wash away my iniquity; cleanse me from my sin." The new translation follows both the word order and the grammar of the Latin text. It is based on Psalm 51:2: "Wash me thoroughly from my iniquity, and cleanse me from my sin."

There is a slight change in the Introduction to the *Orate, Fratres* (pray, brethren).

Previous Translation	New Translation
Pray, brethren, that our sacrifice may be acceptable to God, the almighty Father.	Pray, brethren (brothers and sisters), that my sacrifice and yours may be acceptable to God, the almighty Father.

I imagine most of us will find this new introduction to be an improvement. The reference to "brethren" is a bit archaic for today's people. Rather than simply say "our sacrifice," the new translation underscores that this sacrifice that we are offering is "mine and yours," restoring the emphasis found in the original Latin text of the offering of a single sacrifice.

The response of the people has one minor change. The new translation added an adjective that was omitted in the old translation: "holy" in the phrase "all his *holy* Church." Otherwise, it is the same as the previous translation.

Previous Translation	New Translation
May the Lord accept the sacrifice at your hands for the praise and glory of his name, for our good, and the good of all his Church.	May the Lord accept the sacrifice at your hands for the praise and glory of his name, for our good and the good of all his holy Church.

The Prayer over the Offerings (not "gifts") returns to the original title found in the Latin text: *orationem super oblata*. It also retains the word order of the Latin and translates all the words found in the Latin text, which the previous translations sometimes did not do.

Let me give you an example of what to expect in the new translation of the Prayer over the Offerings:

Previous Translation First Sunday of Lent	New Translation First Sunday of Lent
Lord, make us worthy to bring you these gifts. May this sacrifice help to change our lives. We ask this in the name of Jesus the Lord.	Give us the right dispositions, O Lord, we pray, to make these offerings, for with them we celebrate the beginning of this venerable and sacred time. Through Christ our Lord.

Notice that the reference to God ("O Lord") appears later in the prayer. The previous translation tended to move the mention of God up to the beginning of most prayers. The Latin text has more variety than that. Sometimes, it places God's name at the very beginning of the prayer. As in the example above, it embodies the reference to God after a few words of the prayer have been proclaimed. Notice too that the ending of the prayer is quite different from the old translation, since the new translation makes it a point to translate more literally the Latin text rather than using what was called a "dynamic equivalent."

One of the goals that *Liturgiam authenticam* articulated was to develop a sacred language for our prayer. Hence, the language used in the new translation is more elevated and conveys a stronger sense of reverence, of entering the realm of sacred mysteries. You can see this in the references to "right dispositions" and the celebration of "the beginning / of this venerable and sacred time." When you compare this more literal translation to the previous translation, it is hard to believe that they are translating the same Latin text.

Preface Dialogue

There are two changes in the Preface Dialogue. The first change is the use of the response, "And with your spirit." This was done in order to more accurately translate the Latin text (*et cum spirtu tuo*) and to bring the English translation of this response in line with the major languages used in the liturgy throughout the world. We have already reviewed the rationale for using "And with your spirit" at the beginning of our discussion of the new greetings found in the Introductory Rite. Let's look at the revised Preface Dialogue:

Previous Translation	New Translation
The Lord be with you. R. And also with you.	The Lord be with you. R. And with your spirit.
Lift up your hearts. R. We lift them up to the Lord.	Lift up your hearts. R. We lift them up to the Lord. Let us give thanks to the Lord our God. R. It is right and just.
Let us give thanks to the Lord our God. R. It is right to give him thanks and praise.	

The second change in the Preface Dialogue is a simplification of what ICEL gave us in the previous translation: "It is right to give him thanks and praise." One of the problems with the previous translation is the added words. However, a hallmark of the Roman liturgy is the fact that it is simple, not wordy, and fairly easy to understand. And so, the decision was made to return to the simple, easy-to-understand response found in the Latin: "It is right and just." There is something elegant and appealing in the simple, direct response of the people ("It is right and just"), which the priest repeats at the beginning of the Preface.

The Preface

The new translation of the Preface follows the word order and grammar of the Latin text, returning to the use of "who" clauses and longer sentences than we are used to (at least in some of the Prefaces).

The Prefaces should be practiced before Mass because the new texts can be harder to proclaim. However, the new Prefaces are more accurate and translate *all* the words and phrases found in the Latin text.

It is important to realize that the Preface is the first part or introduction to the Eucharistic Prayer. According to GIRM, 78, the Preface helps people realize that "the meaning of this Prayer is that the whole congregation of the faithful joins with Christ in confessing the great deeds of God and in the offering of Sacrifice. The Eucharistic Prayer requires that everybody listens to it with reverence and in silence."

Let's look at Preface I of Easter (formerly called Easter I), which did not return to the use of the "who" clauses due to the complexity of the Latin text. I chose this example because it illustrates the fact that Rome was willing to compromise on its desire to return to a more literal translation when doing so produced a prayer that was too difficult to comprehend because it had too many different ideas in it. This particular Preface is divided into shorter sentences, while retaining its emphasis on a more literal translation of the Latin text:

Previous Translation	New Translation
Father, all-powerful and ever-living God, we do well always and everywhere to give you thanks through Jesus Christ our Lord. We praise you with greater joy than ever on this Easter night (day) (in this Easter season), when Christ became our paschal sacrifice. He is the true Lamb who took away the sins of the world. By dying he destroyed our death; by rising he restored our life. And so, with all the choirs of angels in heaven we proclaim your glory and join in their unending hymn of praise:	It is truly right and just, our duty and our salvation, at all times to *acclaim* you, O Lord, but (on this night / on this day / in this time) above all to *laud* you yet *more gloriously*, when Christ our Passover has been *sacrificed*. For he is the true Lamb who has taken away the sins of the world; by dying he has destroyed our death, and by rising, restored our life. Therefore, *overcome* with *paschal joy*, *every land, every people* exults in your praise and even the heavenly *Powers*, with the angelic *hosts*, sing together the unending hymn of your *glory*, as they acclaim:

Notice how much of the old prayer was never translated by the previous ICEL translation. The new translation is a restoration of words and phrases from our prayer tradition that the old translation had thrown out.

For example, "To give you thanks" becomes "to laud you yet more gloriously." While some people may not be familiar with the verb *laud*, it is simply another way of saying "praise." People who celebrate Morning Prayer from the Liturgy of the Hours frequently call this prayer "Lauds." Hence, there is a great deal of tradition behind the use of this term. "To laud you yet more gloriously" is trying to express that dimension of the sacred that the more common language of the old translation frequently failed to capture.

"When Christ became our paschal sacrifice" becomes "when Christ our Passover has been sacrificed." The adjective "paschal" is not found in the Latin text. The word used was "Passover," a title given to Jesus.

The conclusion of the Preface in the new translation is much more majestic and joyful-sounding than the simplified conclusion of the previous translation. While it may take priests a little more preparation time, at least initially, to read this prayer in its new translation, the new translation is worth their effort.

"Overcome with paschal joy" is a very evocative phrase. "Every land, every people exults in your praise" was not translated in the previous text. I would rather talk about "heavenly Powers" and "angelic hosts" than simply say "with all the choirs of angels in heaven." The Latin had developed a special, sacred language to express the realities referred to in these prayers. The new translation attempts to express that special language in its choice of words and by translating accurately all the words of the Latin text.

Holy, Holy, Holy

Sometimes, we forget the Biblical connection (Isaiah 6:3) to the first words of the Holy, Holy, Holy. GIRM, 79 reminds us of this when it defines this prayer as "the *acclamation*, by which the whole congregation, joining with the heavenly powers, sings the *Sanctus* (*Holy, Holy, Holy*). This acclamation, which constitutes part of the Eucharistic Prayer itself, is pronounced by all the people with the Priest."

Another prayer that our people sing may pose a bigger challenge than priests having to read the Preface ahead of time. The wording of the Sanctus or Holy, Holy, Holy has been changed at the beginning of the prayer. It will require a minor rewrite of the musical texts that people are used to, but composers assure us that this is not a difficult task. Let's look at the texts.

Previous Translation	New Translation
Holy, holy, holy Lord, God of *power and might*, heaven and earth are full of your glory. Hosanna in the highest. Blessed is he who comes in the name of the Lord. Hosanna in the highest.	Holy, Holy, Holy Lord God of *hosts*. Heaven and earth are full of your glory. Hosanna in the highest. Blessed is he who comes in the name of the Lord. Hosanna in the highest.

The big change in the new translation is in the first line. Where the previous translation had "Holy, holy, holy Lord, God of *power and might*," (emphasis added) the new translation has "Holy, Holy, Holy Lord God of *hosts*" (emphasis added). The new translation follows the punctuation of the Latin, capitalizing the word "Holy" or *Sanctus* and uniting the title "Lord" to God.

Our Bishops avoided using the Latin word *Sabaoth*. Instead they agreed to use the word "hosts," which is much easier to sing and to pronounce. In fact, anyone who still has an old Saint Joseph Missal from the days when Mass was all in Latin will recall that "Lord God of hosts" was the translation used in the old bilingual missals. It is based on a passage in Isaiah 6:3, which reads: "Holy, holy, holy is the Lord of hosts!"

The Eucharistic Prayer

There are so many Eucharistic Prayers that we can use that the discussion of the Eucharistic Prayers requires a separate chapter, which will review all the Eucharistic Prayers found in *The Roman Missal*. Please see Chapter 4 (pp. 84–104) and Chapter 5 (pp. 105–132).

The Communion Rite

In the Communion Rite, the priest now has only one option to introduce the Our Father: "At the Savior's command / and formed by divine teaching, / we dare to say." Rubric number 124 says: "After the chalice and paten have been set down, the Priest, with hands joined, says." This rubric does not give priests permission to make up their own introduction.

In Eucharistic Prayer III we pray that all may be one, as Jesus and the Father are one. We pray that we might become "one body, one spirit in Christ." The one prayer we have from Jesus that expresses his own experience of oneness (communion with God the Father) is the prayer known as the Our Father or the Lord's Prayer. We proclaim the Lord's Prayer at this point as a way to move us ever closer to the moment of the reception of Holy Communion.

The words of the Our Father also fit in nicely with the major themes of the Eucharist. GIRM, 81 reminds us that "In the Lord's Prayer a petition is made for daily bread, which for Christians means principally the Eucharistic Bread, and entreating also purification from sin, so that what is holy may in truth be given to the holy." Jesus, the holy one, will shortly be given to us, his holy people, in the reception of Holy Communion.

Embolism

While there is no change in the wording of the Our Father, there is a change to the prayer that is inserted into the Our Father. This prayer is called the embolism (insertion), and it follows more closely the words in the Latin text. Hence, you will find the adverb "graciously" added to the prayer: "graciously grant peace in our days." Rather than use the word "anxiety," we will now say "we may be . . . safe from all distress." Distress can be internal or external. Anxiety is only internal. We pray at this point to be free from all distress of every kind.

GIRM, 81 states:

> Then the Priest alone adds the embolism, which the people conclude by means of the doxology. The embolism, developing the last petition of the Lord's Prayer itself, asks for deliverance from the power of evil for the whole community of the faithful.

Let's look at the new text of the embolism:

Previous Translation	New Translation
Deliver us, Lord, from every evil, and grant us peace in our day. In your mercy keep us free from sin and protect us from all anxiety as we wait in joyful hope for the coming of our Savior, Jesus Christ.	Deliver us, Lord, we pray, from every evil, graciously grant peace in our days, that, by the help of your mercy, we may be always free from sin and safe from all distress, as we await the blessed hope and the coming of our Savior, Jesus Christ.

Prayer for Peace

The wording of the conclusion to the prayer for peace is more accurately translated as: "and graciously grant her peace and unity / in accordance with your will. / Who live and reign for ever and ever." While the new translation of the prayer for peace is very similar to the old translation, the new translation does a better job of reflecting the biblical text (John 14:27: "Peace I leave with you; my peace I give to you") upon which this prayer is based. Let's look at the two texts.

Previous Translation	New Translation
Lord Jesus Christ, you said to your apostles: I leave you peace, my peace I give you. Look not on our sins, but on the faith of your Church, and grant us the peace and unity of your kingdom, where you live for ever and ever.	Lord Jesus Christ, who said to your Apostles: Peace I leave you, my peace I give you, look not on our sins, but on the faith of your Church, and graciously grant her peace and unity in accordance with your will. Who live and reign for ever and ever.

The Sign of Peace

Like Jesus in the numerous appearance stories in the Gospel (John 20:19), the priest says to the people: "The peace of the Lord be with you always. Let us offer each other the sign of peace." The prayer for peace and its accompanying sign of peace are meant to express the people's "ecclesial communion and mutual charity before communicating in the Sacrament" (GIRM, 82).

Remember that we prayed for unity as "one body, one spirit in Christ" during Eucharistic Prayer III. We also were united as a people in praying the Lord's Prayer, which reflected his unity with (or communion with) God the Father. It is only fitting that we add a visual sign of this unity by exchanging the sign of peace, which can be a handshake, a kiss, a wave, or some other suitable sign.

We need to avoid losing the sense of prayer that we have carefully built up to this point by engaging in a raucous exchange of the sign of peace. GIRM, 82 reminds us of this when it says "it is appropriate that each person, in a sober manner, offer the sign of peace only to those who are nearest." Running around the whole church giving the sign of peace is not what is intended here.

The Breaking of the Bread

While the Lamb of God is sung or recited, the priest, according to rubric number 129, "takes the host, breaks it over the paten, and places a small piece in the chalice, saying quietly: / 'May this mingling of the Body and Blood / of our Lord Jesus Christ / bring eternal life to us who receive it.'" GIRM, 83 further affirms that

> The gesture of breaking bread done by Christ at the
> Last Supper, which in apostolic times gave the entire

Eucharistic Action its name, signifies that the many faithful are made one body (1 Cor. 10:17) by receiving Communion from the One Bread of Life, which is Christ, who for the salvation of the world died and rose again.

While this symbolic gesture of breaking the bread should not be rushed, GIRM, 83 also reminds us: "The fraction or breaking of bread is begun after the sign of peace and is carried out with proper reverence, and should not be unnecessarily prolonged or accorded exaggerated importance."

The Lamb of God

The text of the Lamb of God also remains the same as the previous translation. Of course, the Lamb of God prayer is based on John 1:29, where John the Baptist says: "Behold the Lamb of God, who takes away the sin of the world" (NAB). Rubric number 130 reminds us that the Lamb of God may be repeated several times, if the breaking of the bread is prolonged.

The Priest's Silent Prayers before Receiving Communion

The two silent prayers that the priest says silently before receiving Communion have some minor changes in them, making them more literal and true to the Latin original. In option one, we now have "You gave life to the world through your death" instead of "your death brought life to the world." The reference to Christ's holy body has now restored the superlative of the adjective used. We now have "your most holy Body and Blood." We now mention the commandments explicitly, rather than use the more generic term "teaching." The new translation uses "keep me always faithful to your commandments."

Previous Translation	New Translation
Lord Jesus Christ, Son of the living God, by the will of the Father and the work of the Holy Spirit your death brought life to the world. By your holy body and blood free me from all my sins, and from every evil. Keep me faithful to your teaching, and never let me be parted from you.	Lord Jesus Christ, Son of the living God, who, by the will of the Father and the work of the Holy Spirit, through your Death gave life to the world, free me by this, your most holy Body and Blood, from all my sins and from every evil; keep me always faithful to your commandments, and never let me be parted from you.

Option two has a few more changes. It corrects the wording of the previous translation and follows more closely the word order of the Latin text. Let's look at the differences:

Previous Translation	New Translation
Lord Jesus Christ, with faith in your love and mercy I eat your body and drink your blood. Let it not bring me condemnation, but health in mind and body.	May the receiving of your Body and Blood, Lord Jesus Christ, not bring me to judgment and condemnation, but through your loving mercy be for me protection in mind and body and a healing remedy.

I find a more elegant, reverent, and powerful expression of belief in the effects of receiving Holy Communion expressed in the new translation. The meaning is clearer, more forceful, and more comforting: "keep me always faithful to your commandments /

and never let me be parted from you" or "be for me protection in mind and body / and a healing remedy."

Invitation to Communion and People's Response

According to rubric number 132, "the Priest genuflects, takes the host, and holding it slightly raised above the paten or above the chalice, while facing the people, says aloud" the Invitation to Communion ("Behold the Lamb of God"/*Ecce Agnus Dei*). This prayer has changed slightly to translate more completely the Latin text and to bring out more clearly its biblical references. Let's look at the two texts:

Previous Translation	New Translation
This is the Lamb of God who takes away the sins of the world. Happy are those who are called to his supper.	Behold the Lamb of God, behold him who takes away the sins of the world. Blessed are those called to the supper of the Lamb.

The biblical references in the prayer are strengthened. First, you have "*Behold* the Lamb of God," which is based on John 1:29 (NAB): "*Behold*, the Lamb of God, who takes away the sin of the world." Then you have "*Blessed* are those called to the *supper of the Lamb*" (emphasis added), which is based on Revelation 19:9: "Blessed are those who are invited to the marriage supper of the Lamb."

The response of the people is more faithful to the Latin text and also highlights its biblical roots. Refer to the biblical text of Luke 7:6, where the Roman centurion says to Jesus: "Lord, do not trouble yourself, for I am not worthy to have you come under my roof. Therefore, I did not presume to come to you. But only speak the word, and let my servant be healed." Let's look at the two texts:

Previous Translation	New Translation
Lord, I am not worthy to receive you, but only say the word and I shall be healed.	Lord, I am not worthy that you should enter under my roof, but only say the word and my soul shall be healed.

The new translation restores this connection, is very readable, and is easy to memorize. In fact, if you still have your old Saint Joseph Missal, you will find in it much the same translation that the third edition of *The Roman Missal* now uses. The main difference is that in the Latin Mass, we used to say this prayer three times.

The two private prayers that the priest says quietly (rubric number 133) have only a minor change in the translation of the verb "bring" and the adjective "everlasting":

Previous Translation	New Translation
May the body of Christ *bring me* to everlasting life.	May the Body of Christ *keep me safe* for *eternal* life.
May the blood of Christ bring me to *everlasting* life.	May the Blood of Christ *keep me safe* for *eternal* life.

Receiving Holy Communion

GIRM, 85 reminds us that "it is most desirable that the faithful, just as the Priest himself is bound to do, receive the Lord's Body from hosts consecrated at the same Mass and that, in the cases where this is foreseen, they partake of the chalice, so that even by means of the signs Communion may stand out more clearly as a participation in the sacrifice actually being celebrated."

In other words, we need to avoid consecrating more hosts at Mass than we need. While you will usually have a few hosts left over and placed in the tabernacle, the hosts in the tabernacle are intended for those who are sick or homebound, as well as to facilitate prayer and adoration. At the Last Supper Jesus said, "Take this, all of you, and eat of it" and "Take this, all of you, and drink from it." Jesus would not have said those words and then given out consecrated bread and consecrated wine from a previous celebration. We should follow his good example in avoiding, whenever possible, consecrating too many hosts at any one celebration.

Communion under Both Species

Note, too, that the usual norm for the reception of Holy Communion is Communion under both species: both the consecrated hosts and the consecrated wine, the Body and Blood of Christ. While health concerns may move some people during flu seasons and other times of the year to pass by the reception of Communion from the cup, it should nonetheless be offered to people, since there are no scientific studies that prove you can catch a cold from receiving from the cup. However, we need to respect people's freedom not to receive from the cup, since you receive the whole Christ in either species.

Silent Prayer When Purifying Vessels

As in the previous translation, there is a silent prayer included for the priest or deacon to say when he purifies the paten over the chalice and the chalice itself (see rubric number 137). The new translation more accurately corresponds to the Latin text. Let's look at the two texts:

Previous Translation	New Translation
Lord, may I receive these gifts in purity of heart. May they bring me healing and strength, now and forever.	What has passed our lips as food, O Lord, may we possess in purity of heart, that what has been given to us in time may be our healing for eternity.

Quiet Prayer after Receiving Communion

The same recommendation found in the previous Missal remains in force in the new Missal. GIRM, 88 states: "When the distribution of Communion is over, if appropriate, the Priest and faithful pray quietly for some time." I find that if I sit down and bow my head in prayer for a brief period of personal prayer, most of the people in my congregation also do the same thing. This time for silent prayer can be an important moment to the conclusion of the Eucharistic celebration. In fact, it is often the last quiet minute you have at Mass.

Prayer after Communion

In the Prayers after Communion, the wording continues the same principles that have been applied consistently throughout the new translation. According to GIRM, 89: "To bring to completion the prayer of the People of God, and also to conclude the whole Communion Rite, the Priest pronounces the Prayer after Communion, in which he prays for the fruits of the mystery just celebrated." Let's look at an example from the Prayer after Communion for the Solemnity of Our Lord Jesus Christ, King of the Universe:

Previous Translation	New Translation
Lord, you give us Christ, the King of all creation, as food for everlasting life. Help us to live by his gospel and bring us to the joy of his kingdom, where he lives and reigns for ever and ever.	Having received the food of immortality, we ask, O Lord, that, glorying in obedience to the commands of Christ, the King of the universe, we may live with him eternally in his heavenly Kingdom. Who lives and reigns for ever and ever.

As you can tell from the above example, the new Prayers after Communion adhere more closely to the Latin word order, translate all the words in the Latin text, place the name of God in a variety of places (both at the beginning and somewhere in the middle of the prayer), and end with a "who" clause—"Who lives and reigns for ever and ever." They will require some preparation ahead of time in order to read them well. However, they often have a more poetic sound than the old text. For example, "glorying in obedience / to the commands of Christ" and "we may live with him eternally in his heavenly Kingdom" certainly have a more evocative sense to them than "Help us to live by his gospel / and bring us to the joy of his kingdom."

QUESTIONS FOR CONTINUED REFLECTION

1. What is the purpose of the Preparation of the Gifts?

2. What gifts, vessels, and materials are placed on the altar? What types of gifts does GIRM expressly forbid being placed on the altar?

3. Why do the rubrics indicate that the priest says the two blessing prayers "in a low voice" when the people are singing a hymn?

4. What is the significance of incensing the gifts, the altar, the cross, the priest, and the people? On what special occasions should incense be used?

5. What important prayer in the Mass begins after the priest says the Prayer over the Offerings?

6. What is your reaction to the minor changes in the Preface Dialogue?

7. Do you have any concerns about the wording of the Prefaces used at Mass?

8. Do you welcome the change in the Holy, Holy, Holy to the biblical (Isaiah 6:3) reference to "God of hosts," rather than keeping the old translation, "God of power and might"?

9. Why do we say the Our Father or the Lord's Prayer at the beginning of the Communion Rite?

10. What is the significance of the sign of peace? Have you experienced any problems with the way the sign of peace is done at your church?

11. In the "Lord, I am not worthy" prayer, we now make use of the biblical reference "that you should enter under my roof." Do you see this as an improvement over the old translation of this prayer?

12. What is the value of receiving hosts consecrated at the same Mass, rather than receiving hosts from the tabernacle?

13. How important to you is it to receive Holy Communion under both species?

14. What is the value of taking time for quiet prayer after receiving Holy Communion?

The Concluding Rites

Brief Announcements

Before the final blessing, rubric number 140 says that "if they are necessary, any brief announcements to the people follow here." The "here" referred to is immediately after the Prayer after Communion.

Announcements are meant to be part of the Concluding Rites, if they are necessary. Yet, many parishes insist on having the announcements before the Prayer after Communion. In doing so, they are interrupting the conclusion of the Liturgy of the Eucharist. It is a problem throughout our nation.

If we keep the announcements brief, we can avoid the usual up-and-down routine: stand up for the Prayer after Communion, sit down for the announcements, and then stand for the final blessing. The problem we face in many communities is that people do not read the parish bulletin. So the pastor is under a lot of pressure to announce meetings, fundraisers, social gatherings, registrations for programs, etc. Eventually, you end up reading the parish bulletin to the congregation. Is this really what people need?

With the dawn of e-mail, you can make a concerted effort to send e-mails to the parishioners with the parish bulletin. If it seems necessary, you can also give a one-page summary of important programs and events coming up in the parish. This may lessen some of the pressure on the pastor to allow the long, drawn-out announcements that unfortunately take place all too often.

The Final Blessing

For most Masses, the simple closing blessing is sufficient: "May almighty God bless you, the Father, ✝ and the Son, ✝ and the Holy ✝ Spirit." However, better use could be made of the rich assortment of alternative blessings and prayers over the people found at the end of the Order of Mass.

The section of the Missal titled "Blessings at the End of Mass and Prayers Over the People" includes the following:

- Fourteen Solemn Blessings for different liturgical times, including six Solemn Blessings for Ordinary Time
- Four Solemn Blessings for celebrations of saints: Mary, SS. Peter and Paul, the Apostles, and All Saints
- Two Solemn Blessings: "For the Dedication of a Church" and "In Celebrations for the Dead"
- Twenty-eight Prayers over the People, including two for saints

The Solemn Blessings are identified by their use in different liturgical times: for saints, for the dedication of a church, and for celebrations for the dead. Except for the two Prayers over the People marked out for saints, the other twenty-six options do not identify a time or celebration when they would be appropriate. If we are to make better use of the Prayers over the People, the priest with his liturgy committee will have to identify possible celebrations when a particular Prayer over the People is appropriate.

The *Ordo* (the book which specifies the particular Mass to be celebrated, the readings, the color of vestments, the week we are in for the celebration of the Liturgy of the Hours, etc.) is also a good resource, since suggestions are occasionally made for the use of a Solemn Blessing or one of the Prayers over the People.

The Dismissal

In the Concluding Rites of Mass, there are four options for the priest's or deacon's dismissal of the congregation:

- "Go forth, the Mass is ended." If you say this the wrong way, it can almost sound like you are kicking the people out of church. Priests must be careful if they choose to use this short form of dismissal.
- "Go and announce the Gospel of the Lord." This was introduced as an option by Pope Benedict XVI, who wanted to strengthen the sense of being sent out on mission at the end of each Eucharistic celebration.
- "Go in peace, glorifying the Lord by your life." As we leave the church, we are reminded of the close connection between liturgy and life. Our life, like that of Mary, should proclaim the greatness of God.
- "Go in peace." Simple, short, and elegant, this dismissal reminds us to live in peace with God and each other. The peace referred to here is the Jewish concept of *shalom*, which refers to our sense of holiness and wholeness. Given the many forces at work aiming to destroy our sense of peace, this can be a powerful statement for people to hear prior to leaving the church.

Our Bishops requested that we retain the familiar dismissal: "The Mass is ended. Go in peace to love and serve the Lord." However, this is not found in the Latin text of *The Roman Missal* and consequently was not approved for continued use.

QUESTIONS FOR CONTINUED REFLECTION

1. How do you react to the number and quality of announcements given at the end of Mass in your parish or institution?

2. What solutions do you have for avoiding lengthy announcements, whenever possible?

3. Do you think greater use of e-mails to parishioners might lessen the need for lengthy announcements at Mass?

4. How much use does your parish make of Solemn Blessings and Prayers over the People? Would you like to see more of these options for blessings used at your parish?

5. What is your reaction to the four options for the priest's dismissal of the congregation? Do you like the new options? Why or why not?

6. During the recessional, do you prefer to sing a final hymn, or do you find instrumental music a good option to use occasionally?

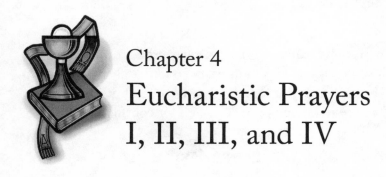

Chapter 4
Eucharistic Prayers
I, II, III, and IV

According to the *General Instruction of the Roman Missal* (GIRM), 30, the Eucharistic Prayer is the high point of the whole Eucharistic celebration: "Among those things assigned to the Priest, the prime place is occupied by the Eucharistic Prayer, which is the high point of the whole celebration."

The Eucharistic Prayer is a *presidential prayer.* The Presidential Prayers reserved to the priest are the Collect, the Prayer over the Offerings, the Preface, the Eucharistic Prayer, and the Prayer after Communion. "These prayers are addressed to God by the Priest who presides over the assembly in the person of Christ, in the name of the entire holy people and of all present. Hence, they are rightly called the 'presidential prayers'" (GIRM, 30).

Eucharistic Prayers *require the attention of the whole congregation.* As GIRM, 32 states: "The nature of the 'presidential' parts requires that they be spoken in a loud and clear voice and that everyone listen to them attentively."

GIRM, 78 defines the Eucharistic Prayer as the "center and high point" of the whole celebration, the great prayer of thanksgiving (the word "Eucharist" means "to give thanks") and personal sanctification. As GIRM, 78 states:

> The Priest calls upon the people to lift up their hearts towards the Lord in prayer and thanksgiving; he associates the people with himself in the Prayer that he

addresses in the name of the entire community to God the Father through Jesus Christ in the Holy Spirit. Furthermore, the meaning of this Prayer is that the whole congregation of the faithful joins with Christ in confessing the great deeds of God and in the offering of Sacrifice. The Eucharistic Prayer requires that everybody listens to it with reverence and in silence.

Note: This is the second time GIRM has called for the congregation to listen attentively, with reverence and in silence, during the Eucharistic Prayer.

In order to accomplish this goal, it is helpful to be familiar with the eight main elements that constitute and are part of our Eucharistic Prayer. To quote GIRM, 79, these eight main elements are:

- *Thanksgiving* (expressed especially in the Preface), in which the Priest, in the name of the whole of the holy people, glorifies God the Father and gives thanks to him for the whole work of salvation or for some particular aspect of it, according to the varying day, festivity, or time of year.
- The *acclamation,* by which the whole congregation, joining with the heavenly powers, sings the *Sanctus* (*Holy, Holy, Holy*). This acclamation, which constitutes part of the Eucharistic Prayer itself, is pronounced by all the people with the Priest.
- The *epiclesis,* in which, by means of particular invocations, the Church implores the power of the Holy Spirit that the gifts offered by human hands be consecrated, that is, become Christ's Body and Blood, and that the unblemished sacrificial Victim to be consumed in Communion may be for the salvation of those who will partake of it.
- The *Institution narrative and Consecration,* by which, by means of the words and actions of Christ, that Sacrifice is effected which Christ himself instituted during the Last Supper, when he offered his Body and Blood under the species of bread and

wine, gave them to the Apostles to eat and drink, and leaving with the latter the command to perpetuate this same mystery.

- The *anamnesis*, by which the Church, fulfilling the command that she received from Christ the Lord through the Apostles, celebrates the memorial of Christ, recalling especially his blessed Passion, glorious Resurrection, and Ascension into heaven.

- The *oblation*, by which, in this very memorial, the Church, in particular that gathered here and now, offers the unblemished sacrificial Victim in the Holy Spirit to the Father. The Church's intention, indeed, is that the faithful not only offer this unblemished sacrificial Victim but also learn to offer their very selves, and so day by day to be brought, through the mediation of Christ, into unity with God and with each other, so that God may at last be all in all.

- The *intercessions*, by which expression is given to the fact that the Eucharist is celebrated in communion with the whole Church, of both heaven and of earth, and that the oblation is made for her and for all her members, living and dead, who are called to participate in the redemption and salvation purchased by the Body and Blood of Christ.

- The *concluding doxology*, by which the glorification of God is expressed and which is affirmed and concluded by the people's acclamation *Amen*.

In every Eucharistic Prayer you will find the preceding elements. Hopefully, by studying the preceding description of each element, you will find it easier to participate in this "high point" of the Mass with increased reverence and attention.

SINGING PARTS OF THE EUCHARISTIC PRAYER

One of the interesting recommendations embodied in rubric number 32 is that "in all Masses, the Priest celebrant is permitted to sing parts of the Eucharistic Prayer provided with musical notion below, pp. 693ff., especially the principal parts" (by this they refer to the consecration of the bread and wine and the doxology). I too want to encourage those able to sing to do so, especially on solemn occasions, like Holy Thursday or the Easter Vigil. It adds a special dimension of festivity to the celebration of the Eucharist that simply speaking the prayer does not have.

Now that we have reviewed the main elements in the Eucharistic Prayer, let's look at the improvements in the translations of the original four Eucharistic Prayers.

EUCHARISTIC PRAYER I

The text we have today for Eucharistic Prayer I (the Roman Canon) evolved into its final form between the end of the fourth and seventh centuries. Since the time of Pope Gregory the Great (c. 604), there have been very few changes in this prayer. Hence, its antiquity is unquestioned.

The Roman Canon was first introduced into England in the seventh century, into Gaul in the eighth century, into Spain in the eleventh century, and into Celtic countries from the ninth to the twelfth centuries.[1] You may be wondering at this point what these countries and others were using as their Eucharistic Prayer.

Until the establishment of the Sacred Congregation of Rites in 1588, there were no universally mandated Eucharistic Prayers that had to be said. Local Churches were free to use whatever texts they had at their disposal. In a study of some of the better-known Eucharistic Prayers contained in the book *Prex Eucharistica*,[2] you can find over a hundred texts for Eucharistic Prayers in languages such as Greek, Latin, and various Oriental (Eastern Rite) languages. For example, you can read the famous *Canon Dominicus Papae Gelasii*, the Eucharistic Prayer attributed to Pope Gelasius (d. 496).

---

1. See Enrico Mazza, *The Eucharistic Prayers of the Roman Rite* (New York: Pueblo Publishing Company, 1986), p. 53.

2. Anton Hänggi and Irmgard Pahl, eds., *Prex Eucharistica: Textus e Variis Liturgiis Antiquioribus Selecti* (Switzerland: Éditions Universitaires Fribourg Suisse, 1968).

Until the Sacred Congregation of Rites began to mandate that all Western Rites use the Roman Canon found in the Latin *Missale Romanum*, there was a great deal of variety in terms of the Eucharistic Prayers prayed at the Eucharist. Vatican II returned to the original tradition of providing multiple Eucharistic Prayers for Latin Rite Christians due to the fact that the richness of our Roman Rite traditions cannot be captured in only one Eucharistic Prayer (the venerable Roman Canon).

The new translation of Eucharistic Prayer I follows the Latin word order and punctuation more closely than the previous translation. This is obvious from the very beginning of the Prayer:

Previous Translation	New Translation
We come to you, Father, with praise and thanksgiving, through Jesus Christ your Son.	To you, therefore, most merciful Father, we make humble prayer and petition through Jesus Christ, your Son, our Lord.

Even in this brief excerpt, you can see the type of changes that the new translation will make in all the Eucharistic Prayers:

- Follow the Latin word order
- Follow the Latin punctuation
- Translate all the words (for example, "most merciful," "therefore," "our Lord")

It's amazing how many words from the Latin text the previous translation never translated. Practically every paragraph of Eucharistic Prayer I has examples of this.

The Eucharistic Prayers read very easily, but they contain new words that priests are not used to. In addition, even when the words are the same as the previous edition of *The Roman Missal*, the familiar words are often in different places in the sentence. We need to be patient as our priests gain familiarity with the new words and the placement of old familiar words and phrases.

A good example of the new wording and phrasing found in Eucharistic Prayer I is the beginning of the *Communicantes*, where we recall our union with the saints:

Previous Translation	New Translation
In union with the whole Church we honor Mary, the ever-virgin mother of Jesus Christ our Lord and God.	In communion with those whose memory we venerate, especially the glorious ever-Virgin Mary, Mother of our God and Lord, Jesus Christ, . . .

There is a clearer and more majestic sense in the new translation to our veneration of Mary. It also reintroduces to the people the important distinction that we worship God, but venerate the saints.

There are special *Communicantes* for the Nativity of the Lord and throughout the Octave of Christmas, the Epiphany of the Lord, the Mass of the Easter Vigil until the Second Sunday of Easter, the Ascension of the Lord, and Pentecost Sunday. There is no special *Communicantes* prayer for Holy Thursday, since the one we had was a new text added by ICEL and not found in the Latin text of *The Roman Missal*.

The new translation has eliminated the two alternative versions of the "Bless and approve our offering" that the previous translation provided for Holy Thursday and for the Easter Vigil until the Second Sunday of Easter. They have also eliminated the alternative version of the *Qui, pridie quam pateretur* ("Who on the day before he was to suffer") prayer before the words of Consecration that the previous translation provided for Holy Thursday. They were never part of the Latin text of *The Roman Missal*, but an addition made by ICEL.

While the new translation of the Institution narratives of all the Eucharistic Prayers is similar to the old translation, there are a few minor corrections of the English translation, which should not cause any big upset in the congregation.

In the Consecration of the bread, the new translation adds the preposition "of": "Take this, all of you, and eat *of* it." The preposition (*ex*) was not translated in the previous translation. They also added the word "for," in Latin, *enim*, which was not translated in the previous translation.

Previous Translation	New Translation
Take this, all of you, and eat it: this is my body which will be given up for you.	TAKE THIS, ALL OF YOU, AND EAT *OF* IT, *FOR* THIS IS MY BODY, WHICH WILL BE GIVEN UP FOR YOU.

In the Consecration of the wine, they added the adverb "for" in order to translate the Latin word *enim*, which was not translated in the previous translation. And so the new translation reads: "Take this, all of you, and drink from it, *for* this is the chalice of my Blood" (emphasis added).

Some people will note the introduction of the word "chalice" instead of "cup" when translating the Latin word *calix*. In most Latin dictionaries, "chalice" is the first meaning ascribed to the word *calix*. Moreover, it is more consistent to use "chalice" rather than "cup," since most people speak of the "priest's" chalice used at Mass. "Chalice" better conveys the special quality of the vessel holding the precious Blood than the more generic word "cup."

There is a minor change in the adjective modifying "covenant." Instead of "*everlasting* covenant" (emphasis added), we now have "*eternal* covenant" (emphasis added). The thought was that "eternal" would be easier to sing and made for a more poetic text.

There is another minor word change in the Consecration of the wine. They changed the verb "it will *be shed*" to "it will be *poured out*" (emphasis added). The phrase now reads: "It will be poured out for you and for many." "Pour out" is a stronger metaphor than "shed." The word *men* has been eliminated in the interest of inclusivity, but that is nothing new.

The use of the word "many" in "which will be poured out for you and for many" may at first sound strange. Didn't Jesus die for all people? Yes, that is true. However, Jesus does not force the gift of salvation on all people. We are free to reject it. The words in Latin are *pro multis*, which mean "for many." If the Latin text wanted to say "for all," the words would have been *pro omnibus*. The new translation is thus more accurate than the previous translation was. After all, Jesus himself used the word "many" at the Last Supper.

The reference to the *forgiveness of sins* has been simplified. We now have "for the forgiveness of sins" rather than "so that sins may be forgiven." Let's look at the two texts:

Previous Translation	New Translation
Take this, all of you, and drink from it: this is the cup of my blood, the blood of the new and everlasting covenant. It will be shed for you and for all so that sins may be forgiven. Do this in memory of me.	TAKE THIS, ALL OF YOU, AND DRINK FROM IT, *FOR* THIS IS THE CHALICE OF MY BLOOD, THE BLOOD OF THE NEW AND *ETERNAL* COVENANT; WHICH WILL BE *POURED OUT* FOR YOU AND FOR MANY *FOR THE FORGIVENESS OF SINS.* DO THIS IN MEMORY OF ME.

These same words of Consecration are used in the translation of all the Eucharistic Prayers. While there are minor changes in the wording of the preceding prayers which the priest proclaims, there are some major changes in the Memorial Acclamations.

The introduction to the Memorial Acclamation has been simplified. Instead of saying "Let us proclaim the mystery of faith," we simply have "The mystery of faith." The Latin text never had the words "let us proclaim" in it. This was something that ICEL added. The Latin text was always just two words: *Mysterium fidei.*

The parallel here is with the ending of a scripture reading. Rather than say: "This is the Word of the Lord," we now simply say, "The Word of the Lord." In Latin, the text was always just two words: *Verbum Domini.* This is the way the Latin text brings to a close a major part of the Mass. This simplified approach has now been restored for the Memorial Acclamation. This will probably not be difficult for the congregation. However, as celebrants, it will take a little time for priests to get used to not saying: "Let us proclaim."

What will take more effort getting used to is the fact that we restored a more literal translation of all the Memorial Acclamations, so that they do not read like the previous acclamations read. Let's look at the previous and the new Memorial Acclamations:

Previous Translation	New Translation
A. Christ has died, Christ is risen, Christ will come again.	Not found in the new translation, due to the fact that it is not in the Latin text of *The Roman Missal.*
B. Dying you destroyed our death, rising you restored our life, Lord Jesus, come in glory.	We proclaim your Death, O Lord, and profess your Resurrection until you come again. [*See 1 Corinthians 11:26.*]

C. When we eat this bread and drink this cup, we proclaim your death, Lord Jesus, until you come in glory.	When we eat this Bread and drink this Cup, we proclaim your Death, O Lord, until you come again. [*See 1 Corinthians 11:26.*]
D. Lord, by your cross and resurrection you have set us free. You are the Savior of the world.	Save us, Savior of the world, for by your Cross and Resurrection you have set us free. [*See John 4:42.*]

One fact that had to be faced in the new translation was that at times the previous translation of the Memorial Acclamations was rather loose. In addition, there has been a big effort made to restore the biblical and patristic references obscured by the previous translation. The approach of dynamic equivalence that ICEL used in the past eliminated an easy comparison to famous passages from scripture and the Church Fathers. Consequently, the new translation, while it sounds different, is really more accurate, more faithful to the Latin text and to the biblical and patristic sources that originally inspired the Latin text.

The new translation of the doxology has also followed the word order and syntax of the Latin text, although it is close to the previous translation. Let's look at the texts:

Previous Translation	New Translation
Through him, with him, in him, in the unity of the Holy Spirit, all glory and honor is yours, almighty Father, for ever and ever.	Through him, *and* with him, *and* in him, O God, almighty Father, in the unity of the Holy Spirit, all glory and honor is yours, for ever and ever.

In order to be consistent, we had to change the word order and wording of the new translation to bring out more accurately the flavor of the Latin text.

The Latin text always had the conjunction *et*, or "and," in the first line. ICEL never included it in the first translation. The reference to "God, almighty Father" was always before, not after, the reference to the "unity of the Holy Spirit." The verb *est* or "is" has been moved closer to the adverb modifying it: "for ever and ever," which was always at the end of the prayer. Other language groups retained the word order and the original wording. Now we are in harmony with the rest of the Church.

Eucharistic Prayer II

While some people think of Eucharistic Prayer II as an entirely new composition, it actually is based on an ancient text, the Anaphora of Saint Hippolytus, composed around 215 to 220. Due to its Roman origin, this Eucharistic Prayer enjoyed great renown and influenced the development of the Ethiopian, Syrian, and Antiochene anaphoras.[3] As a result of its prominence as a source for other Eucharistic Prayers, the commission charged with the implementation of the *Constitution on the Sacred Liturgy* chose to remain close to the actual text found in the writings of Saint Hippolytus, known as *The Apostolic Tradition*.

Eucharistic Prayer II begins with a literal and poetic translation of the Latin text:

Previous Translation	Previous Translation
Lord, you are holy indeed, the fountain of all holiness. Let your Spirit come upon these gifts to make them holy.	You are indeed Holy, O Lord, the fount of all holiness. Make holy, therefore, these gifts, we pray, by sending down your Spirit upon them like the dewfall, ...

3. See Mazza, p. 90. Note that the Eastern Church uses the word "anaphora" to describe its Eucharistic Prayers.

While the new translation sometimes sounds more formal than the previous translation, this is a result of returning to the rich metaphors and doctrinal clarity of the original Latin text. A good example of this is found in the second part of the Eucharistic Prayer after the Memorial Acclamation:

Previous Translation	New Translation
In memory of his death and resurrection, we offer you, Father, this life-giving bread, this saving cup. We thank you for counting us worthy to stand in your presence and serve you. May all of us who share in the body and blood of Christ be brought together in unity by the Holy Spirit.	Therefore, as we celebrate the memorial of his Death and Resurrection, we offer you, Lord, the Bread of life and the Chalice of salvation, giving thanks that you have held us worthy to be in your presence and minister to you. Humbly we pray that, partaking of the Body and Blood of Christ, we may be gathered into one by the Holy Spirit.

The new translation restores the use of the term "memorial," which is often used in other Eucharistic Prayers and in the writings of the Fathers of the Church to describe one of the main elements of the Eucharistic Prayer. The "Bread of life" is an obvious biblical reference, obscured by the previous translation's use of the term "life-giving bread." Rather than speak of a "saving cup," the new translation restores the reference to "Chalice of salvation." "Chalice of salvation" is a stronger expression of the doctrine being recalled at this point in the prayer.

Since the Latin text only referred to "being" in God's presence, not standing in God's presence, we now have a stronger unity of the concepts of "being" in God's presence and "ministering" to God. To "minister" has a stronger biblical connection than the more generic verb "serve." You hear overtones of priests ministering to God. Of course, we are a "royal priesthood" offering God our thanksgiving and praise (see Deuteronomy 18:6–7).

There seems to be a stronger sense of reverence when we pray "Humbly we pray / that, partaking of the Body and Blood of Christ." The previous translation never translated the word *supplices* or "humbly." "To *partake* of the Body and Blood of Christ" (emphasis added) sounds more special, more sacred than simply "sharing the body and blood of Christ." "Gathered into one" preserves overtones of Christ's prayer: "May they all be one" (John 17:11).

Throughout this prayer, changes like this will necessitate some study by our priests before they recommit this prayer to memory. With a little preparation, priests will find this new prayer as comfortable and easy to say as the old prayer. The reintroduction of Latin metaphors, the stronger connection to biblical texts, and a more sacral liturgical language will hopefully make this beautiful prayer even more effective in mediating our experience of communion with God.

EUCHARISTIC PRAYER III

Eucharistic Prayer III has become very popular with priests and people, especially for use on Sundays and feast days. One reason for this popularity is that it contains some powerful metaphors that have resonated strongly with people's experience of their faith. These metaphors have not only been preserved but improved in the new translation.

Eucharistic Prayer III takes its inspiration from an Oriental Anaphora, which combines elements of both Antiochene and Alexandrian Eucharistic Prayers. Some scholars describe this Eucharistic Prayer as "the Canon of openness to the world." Others see the emphasis on sacrifice as a defining characteristic.

Many attribute a good deal of the composition of this anaphora to the work of Cipriano Vagaggini, who served on the

Roman commission that produced the official text of this prayer. Vagaggini says it is based in part on the *Anaphor of Theodore of Mospuestia*. It also mirrors the theology found in Saint Paul's Letter to the Romans 12:1. Since Pope Paul VI actively supported the work of the commission that composed this prayer, it is sometimes called the "Canon of Pope Paul VI."[4]

The new translation of Eucharistic Prayer III follows the Latin word order, syntax, and sentence structure. One of the reasons it sounds different from the prayer that we are used to is because ICEL more freely interpolated in the previous translation the word order of the Latin text and added words not found in the Latin text.

Let's look at the beginning of Eucharistic Prayer III:

Previous Translation	New Translation
Father, you are holy indeed, and all creation rightly gives you praise. All life, all holiness comes from you through your Son, Jesus Christ our Lord, by the working of the Holy Spirit. From age to age you gather a people to yourself, so that from east to west a perfect offering may be made to the glory of your name.	You are indeed Holy, O Lord, and all you have created rightly gives you praise, for through your Son our Lord Jesus Christ, by the power and working of the Holy Spirit, you give life to all things and make them holy, and you never cease to gather a people to yourself, so that from the rising of the sun to its setting a pure sacrifice may be offered to your name.

The new translation is more literal and conveys the meaning of the Latin text. The previous translation was more interpretative:

---

4. Mazza, pp. 124–125.

"All life, all holiness comes from you" rather than "you give life to all things and make them holy," which is really what the Latin text says. The Latin text did not mention "from age to age," which was an ICEL addition. And so, the new translation simply says "you never cease to gather a people to yourself." Simplicity and eloquence is a characteristic of Roman Eucharistic Prayers.

Gone is the reference to "from east to west" and instead you read "from the rising of the sun to its setting." The Latin text never referred to "from east to west." The previous translation used a geographical reference, whereas the Latin text refers to time: "from the rising of the sun to its setting." This new translation brings out more clearly the intended emphasis on the fact that every day we offer a pure sacrifice to God. Adding the adjective "pure" rather than "perfect" before the word "sacrifice" again brings out a biblical connection and reintroduces the concept of "purity" to this prayer.

The attention to a more literal translation of our prayer texts and the translation of all the words in Latin has led to a slight reworking of the ending of this Eucharistic Prayer, without losing the metaphors that we have come to love in this prayer.

Previous Translation	New Translation
Lord, may this sacrifice, which has made our peace with you, advance the peace and salvation of all the world. Strengthen in faith and love your pilgrim Church on earth; your servant, Pope N., our bishop N., and all the bishops,	May this Sacrifice of our reconciliation, we pray, O Lord, advance the peace and salvation of all the world. Be pleased to confirm in faith and charity your pilgrim Church on earth, with your servant N. our Pope and N. our Bishop,

with the clergy and the entire people your Son has gained for you. Father, hear the prayers of the family you have gathered here before you. In mercy and love unite all your children wherever they may be.	the Order of Bishops, all the clergy, and the entire people you have gained for your own. Listen graciously to the prayers of this family, whom you have summoned before you: in your compassion, O merciful Father, gather to yourself all your children scattered throughout the world.

One of the benefits of translating all the words in Latin is that you frequently enrich the prayer by restoring obvious biblical connections. This section of the prayer begins with the strong reference to "this Sacrifice of our reconciliation." Reconciliation is a key concept in the Letters of Saint Paul. It is unfortunate that the old translation neglected to translate it.

"Be pleased to confirm in faith and charity" has a more poetic sound to it than the previous translation: "Strengthen in faith and love." The choice of "confirm" to translate the Latin verb *firmare* opens up new connotations not found in the old translation (e.g., connections with the Sacrament of Confirmation), where God confirms our faith. The use of the noun "charity" provides some variety in translating the Latin word *caritate*.

The reference to the "Order of Bishops" has been restored in the new translation. The adverb "graciously" makes the request of God to "Listen graciously to the prayers of this family" richer and fuller. Rather than speak of the congregation simply as "*the* family" (emphasis added), the new translations refers to "*this* family" (emphasis added) because it translates all the words in the

Latin text. The image of "this family, / whom you have summoned before you" is far richer than the rather flat statement "the / family you have gathered here before you." Being summoned has a sense of urgency that being "gathered" does not convey.

The prayer ends with the restoration of an important adjective modifying the noun "Father": "merciful." By not translating this adjective, the old translation did not adequately convey the depth of meaning found in the Latin text. In addition, the old translation added a geographical reference, "wherever they may be," which is not found in the Latin text. Once again, the hallmark of the Latin tradition of prayer is simplicity and eloquence. This is what the new translation hopes to restore.

EUCHARISTIC PRAYER IV

Eucharistic Prayer IV is probably the least used of the four primary Eucharistic Prayers. One reason for this is that it had a problem with inclusive language, was very theoretical, and was difficult to read. The new translation hopes to attend to some of these criticisms.

Eucharistic Prayer IV is the most theological of all our Eucharistic Prayers, praising God for and narrating the history of salvation. It is based on Syro-Antiochene anaphoras, while adding an epiclesis from the Alexandrian liturgy.[5]

Four times Eucharistic Prayer IV refers to God as "holy Father," echoing the classical beginning of many Prefaces as well as using a term with rich biblical connections (see Psalm 68:5; John 17:11). In celebrating the praise of God, Eucharistic Prayer IV refers to God as "one, living, true, good, source of life, great, most holy, almighty, Lord, Creator, Father." As a result, some commentators see Eucharistic Prayer IV as a celebration of God and salvation history.

Eucharistic Prayer IV had such a strong emphasis on the word "men" that some women complained that they felt excluded

---

5. Mazza, p. 158.

when this prayer was used. This problem has been partially dealt with in the new translation, which reads even more smoothly than the previous translation. It restores the meaning of the Latin text in the places where the previous translation departed too much from the Latin original.

Let's look at the beginning of Eucharistic Prayer IV:

Previous Translation	New Translation
Father, we acknowledge your greatness: all your actions show your wisdom and love. You formed man in your own likeness and set him over the whole world to serve you, his creator, and to rule over all creatures. Even when he disobeyed you and lost your friendship you did not abandon him to the power of death, but helped all men to seek and find you. Again and again you offered a covenant to man, and through the prophets taught him to hope for salvation.	We give you praise, Father most holy, for you are great and you have fashioned all your works in wisdom and in love. You formed *man* in your own image and entrusted the whole world to *his* care, so that in serving you alone, the Creator, *he* might have dominion over all creatures. And when through disobedience *he* had lost your friendship, you did not abandon *him* to the domain of death. For you came in mercy to the aid of all, so that those who seek might find you. Time and again you offered them covenants and through the prophets taught them to look forward to salvation.

There are so many changes in wording and word order that the new translation almost sounds like a different prayer and, in many ways, it is a different prayer. It translates all the words in the Latin text, not eliminating words or giving us fanciful translations. For example, the new translation uses "Father most holy" rather than simply saying "Father." "But helped all men to seek and find you" really reflects the words that are found in the Latin text: "For you came in mercy to the aid of all." The previous translation doesn't mention the mercy of God, but it is in the Latin text. The new translation puts back the reference to the mercy of God.

The problem the translators faced with the issue of inclusive language was the fact that the line "you formed man in your own image" is a direct reference to a quote from Genesis 1:26: "Then God said, 'Let us make *mankind* in our image, according to our likeness. . .'" (emphasis added). If you retain the obvious connection with Genesis 1:26, which refers to creating man in God's image and likeness, then for the sake of consistency you have to use male references in many of the references that immediately follow this sentence (see the italicized texts above).

Some people suggested that concerns about inclusivity should lead translators to translate the Latin word *hominem* as "men and women," not simply as "man." This was hotly debated, and the decision was made that using "men and women" interfered with the poetry of the text and did not faithfully convey the biblical text upon which it is based. However, in the second half of the prayer, you do find inclusivity:

> For you came in mercy to the aid of *all*,
> so that *those* who seek might find you.
> Time and again you offered *them* covenants
> and through the prophets
> taught *them* to look forward to salvation.

And so the issue of inclusivity remains a problem for some people, despite some improvements in the new translation of the text.

Part of the reason the new translation of Eucharistic Prayer IV sounds different from the previous translation is that it follows the new norms for translation which mandate greater attention to the wording of the Latin text, translating all the words and metaphors found in the Latin, as well as attempting to develop a special language, suitable for divine worship. A good example of this occurs in the second part of Eucharistic Prayer IV after the Memorial Acclamation:

Previous Translation	New Translation
Lord, look upon this sacrifice which you have given to your Church; and by your Holy Spirit, gather all who share this one bread and one cup into the one body of Christ, a living sacrifice of praise.	Look, O Lord, upon the Sacrifice which you yourself have provided for your Church, and grant in your loving kindness to all who partake of this one Bread and one Chalice that, gathered into one body by the Holy Spirit, they may truly become a living sacrifice in Christ to the praise of your glory.

The new translation follows the word order of the Latin, by beginning with the verb "look" and then addressing God, "O Lord." The second line talks about God as a good provider: "you yourself have provided for your Church"—a wonderful image that was lost in the previous translation: "you have given to your Church."

The new translation restores the reference to God's "loving kindness," which was omitted in the previous translation. Rather than simply speak about sharing the bread and wine, the new translation talks about partaking "of this one Bread and one Chalice." The previous translation refers to "cup," when the word used in Latin, *calix*, is the word "Chalice." The new translation makes it clearer that the gathering of God's people into one body is the work of the Holy Spirit. The new translation adds at the

end of the paragraph a reference omitted in the previous translation: "to the praise of your glory."

In short, while Eucharistic Prayer IV sounds different
than the previous prayer, it is fairly easy to read and makes clear
the biblical connections and Latin metaphors. The success of the
attempt to develop a sacral language for worship in the new
translation will only be evident after years of use.

QUESTIONS FOR CONTINUED REFLECTION

1. Why does GIRM identify the Eucharistic Prayer as the
    high point of the whole celebration?

2. What are the main parts found in every Eucharistic
    Prayer? Do you have any questions about a particular
    part of the Eucharistic Prayer?

3. Do you support priests singing parts of the Eucharistic
    Prayer? Why or why not?

4. What is your reaction to the changes made in the trans-
    lation of Eucharistic Prayer I?

5. Do you understand the rationale behind the changes
    made in the Institution narrative?

6. How hard do you think it will be to adjust to the new
    wording of the Memorial Acclamations?

7. What is your reaction to the more literal and poetic
    translation of Eucharistic Prayer II?

8. What is your reaction to the more literal and poetic
    translation of Eucharistic Prayer III?

9. What is your reaction to the more literal and poetic
    translation of Eucharistic Prayer IV?

Chapter 5
Eucharistic Prayers for Reconciliation I and II and Eucharistic Prayers for Use in Masses for Various Needs and Occasions

In this chapter I will cover the two Eucharistic Prayers for Reconciliation and the four Eucharistic Prayers that can be used in Masses for Various Needs:

- The Church on the Path of Unity
- God Guides His Church along the Way of Salvation
- Jesus, The Way to the Father
- Jesus, the One Who Went About Doing Good

EUCHARISTIC PRAYER FOR RECONCILIATION I

The Eucharistic Prayers for Reconciliation were issued by Rome during the Holy Year of 1975, whose theme was reconciliation. They were promulgated along with the Eucharistic Prayers for Children. Since Holy Years have always had a penitential character, the year for reconciliation with God and his people seemed appropriate as an occasion to introduce special Eucharistic Prayers on this theme.

While the Holy See intended these two Eucharistic Prayers to be used on an experimental basis, they have been so well received that Rome has agreed to include them on a

permanent basis as part of *The Roman Missal* itself. Since the
Eucharistic Prayers for Reconciliation are meant to be used with
their own Preface, priests should not use these Eucharistic
Prayers on days when the feast mandates a special Preface.

The texts of the Eucharistic Prayers for Children have
yet to be revised and approved by Rome. The texts of the new
edition of *The Roman Missal* are to be implemented on November
27, 2011. After that date, we will no longer be able to use the
Eucharistic Prayers for Children that are current at this writing,
since they do not contain the new texts confirmed for the
Institution narrative, the Memorial Acclamation, and the doxology. The current plan is to release the revised Eucharistic Prayers
for Children as a separate publication, separate from the texts in
the third edition of *The Roman Missal*.

The same principles that inform the translation of the
first four Eucharistic Prayers of *The Roman Missal* have been
applied to Eucharistic Prayer for Reconciliation I. And so, it will
not be a surprise to see the following:

- Restoration of the Latin word order and syntax
- Use of a few "who" clauses
- Restoration of clearer biblical and patristic references
- Restoration of words and phrases not found in the old
  translation

You can see the application of these principles in the
Preface, where the problems of not following the Latin word
order and hiding the richness of the language found in the Latin
text are quite apparent:

Previous Translation	New Translation
Father, all-powerful and ever-living God, we do well always *and every-where* to give you thanks *and praise.*	It is truly right and just that we should always give you thanks, *Lord, holy* Father, almighty and eternal God.

You never cease to call us to a *new* and more abundant life. *God of love and mercy,* you are always ready to forgive; we are sinners, and you invite us to trust in your mercy. Time and time again we broke your covenant, but you did not abandon us. *Instead*, through your Son, Jesus our Lord, *you bound yourself even more closely to the human family* by a bond that can never be broken.	For you do not cease to spur us on *to possess* a more abundant life and, being rich in mercy, you constantly offer pardon and call on sinners to trust in your forgiveness *alone*. Never did you *turn away* from us, and, though time and again we have broken your covenant, you have *bound the human family to yourself* through Jesus your Son, our Redeemer, with a new bond *of love* so tight that it can never be undone.

The new translation is sufficiently different that it almost sounds like a new prayer. It will take us some time to get used to it. There are new words that the old translation failed to translate and a word order that will be a challenge to read comfortably. Yet it is more accurate and true to the Latin original.

Look first at the previous translation. I have italicized all of the words that ICEL added that are not found in the Latin text. Then look at the new translation. I have italicized a large number of words that the previous translation simply did not translate. This kind of inconsistency in accurately translating the Latin text separated the English translation of *The Roman Missal* from the more literal and accurate translations used by other mainline languages (French, German, Italian, Spanish, etc.). With the new English translation of *The Roman Missal*, there will be a greater universality of translation, regardless of the language that is used around the world.

The previous translation starts out by omitting the reference to "Lord" and the adjective "holy" to modify "Father." Then it adds words not found in the Latin text: "God of love and mercy." It neglects the Latin word order by saying "you bound yourself even more closely to the human family," when the Latin text really says: "you have bound the human family to yourself." While some people may find this distinction irrelevant, the new translation does preserve the logic of the Latin text.

It is not God who is "bound," but rather it is God who does the binding. It is the human family that is bound to God. That is what the Latin text is trying to say. At the end of this prayer, the previous translation omits the reference to the bond "of love" that can never be undone. The previous translation simply says "by a bond that can never be broken." Yet the meaning of the Latin text is more precise and far richer when you add "of love" after "bond." There is a personal sense of affection conveyed by "of love" which using the single word "bond" does not fully convey.

Another example of how different the translation of Eucharistic Prayer for Reconciliation I is can be seen in the *Memores* prayer immediately after the Memorial Acclamation:

Previous Translation	New Translation
We do this in memory of Jesus Christ, our Passover and our *lasting* peace. We celebrate his death and resurrection and look for the coming of *that day* *when he will return to give us the fullness of joy.* Therefore we offer you, God ever faithful and *true*, the sacrifice which *restores man to your friendship.*	Therefore, as we celebrate the memorial of your son Jesus Christ, who is our Passover and our *surest* peace, we celebrate his Death and Resurrection *from the dead*, and looking *forward* to his *blessed* Coming, we offer you, who are our faithful and *merciful* God, this sacrificial *Victim* who *reconciles* to you *the human race.*

Look at the italicized words in the previous translation. They refer to words that are either mistranslated or to additions made by ICEL not found in the Latin text. Now look at the italicized words in the new translation. They refer to words in the Latin text that were either not accurately translated or were eliminated in the old translation.

Where the previous translation refers to our "lasting peace," the new translation more accurately refers to our "surest peace," thus preserving both the superlative sense of the adjective and restoring a metaphor that will engage people today. Peace in our modern world is anything but secure or sure. Specifying that Jesus rose "from the dead" adds greater emphasis to the mention of his Resurrection.

"Looking forward to his blessed Coming" contains the sense of yearning for the return of the Lord, which is inadequately conveyed by "look for the coming of that day." By translating the adjective "blessed," the new translation underscores the special blessing that the second coming of Christ will bring to God's people. "This sacrificial Victim" provides a more adequate translation of the important doctrine of Christ being the sacrificial victim offered to the Father. Simply to say "the sacrifice" impoverishes the understanding of this text.

While "restores man to your friendship" sounds good, it again is inaccurate. It fails to use the important verb "reconciles" with all its rich biblical connotations. The previous translation also uses the word "man," when the Latin is much more inclusive, using "human race." The Latin word here is *homines*, meaning "mankind." If the Latin wanted to use the male noun "man," it would have used the Latin word *vir*. Since the translators wanted to avoid the problem of exclusivity, it avoided all the derivatives of "man," such as "mankind." Instead, it correctly translates *hominem* as "human race."

I believe the changes made in the new translation strengthen our understanding of the true meaning of this prayer by accurately translating the Latin text, including all the words found in the Latin, and avoiding the addition of new words not found in the Latin original.

EUCHARISTIC PRAYER
FOR RECONCILIATION II

Like the preceding Eucharistic Prayer, the differences from the previous translation are very apparent in the Preface of the Eucharistic Prayer for Reconciliation II:

Previous Translation	New Translation
Father, all-powerful and ever-living God, we praise and thank you through Jesus Christ our Lord for your *presence* and action in the world.	It is truly right and just that we should give you thanks and praise, O God, almighty Father, for all *you do* in *this* world, through our Lord Jesus Christ.
In the midst of conflict and division, we know it is you *who turn our minds to thoughts of peace.*	For though the human race is divided by dissension and discord, yet we know that *by testing us you* change our hearts to *prepare them for reconciliation.*
Your Spirit *changes* our hearts: enemies begin to speak to one another, *those who were estranged* join hands *in friendship*, and *nations* seek the way of peace together.	Even more, by your Spirit you *move* human hearts that enemies may speak to each other *again*, *adversaries* join hands, and *peoples* seek to meet together.
Your Spirit is at work when *understanding* puts an end to *strife*, when hatred is quenched *by mercy*, and vengeance gives way to forgiveness.	By the working of your power it comes about, O Lord, that *hatred* is overcome by *love*, revenge gives way to forgiveness, and *discord is changed to mutual respect.*

Read the italicized words in the previous translation. They identify words that were either inaccurately translated from the Latin or were new compositions not found in the Latin text, for example, "who turn our minds to thoughts of peace." Now read the italicized words in the new translation. They point out all the words that the previous translation did not translate, for example, "and discord is changed to mutual esteem." When contemporary translators criticized the liberties taken in the previous translation, they had good reason for making such criticisms.

The new translation introduces some new words and phrases that will resonate easily with people:

- The human race / is divided by dissension and discord.
- You change our hearts / to prepare them for reconciliation.
- By your Spirit, you move human hearts.
- Enemies may speak to each other again.
- Adversaries join hands.
- Hatred is overcome by love.
- Discord is changed to mutual respect.

Consequently, the new translation retains the poetic beauty of the previous translation, while adhering more closely to the Latin text.

Let's look at the *Memores* prayer immediately after the Memorial Acclamation:

Previous Translation	New Translation

Lord our God,
your Son has entrusted to us
this pledge of his love.
We celebrate the memory of
   his death and resurrection
and bring you the gift you
   have given us,
	Celebrating, therefore, the
	   memorial
	of the Death and Resurrection of
	   your Son,
	who left us this pledge of his love,
	we offer you what you *have*
	   bestowed on us,

the sacrifice of reconciliation. Therefore, we ask you, Father, to accept us, together with your Son. Fill us with his Spirit through our sharing in *this meal.* May he take away all that divides us.	the Sacrifice of *perfect* reconciliation. *Holy* Father, we humbly beseech you to accept us *also,* together with your Son, and in this *saving banquet graciously to endow* us with his *very* Spirit, who takes away everything that *estranges us from one another.*

While the previous translation does a fairly good job of accurately translating the Latin text, it does eliminate some words found in the Latin text. See the italicized words in the new translation above. At the same time, the previous translation sometimes uses words that, while technically correct, do not capture the full meaning of the Latin text.

When we say "we offer you what you have bestowed on us," we hear a much richer metaphor than the rather flat statement "and bring you the gift you have given us." Having something "bestowed" on us carries connotations of a special gift or sacred inheritance, the gift of the sacrifice of perfect reconciliation explained in the next phrase.

To speak of a "saving banquet" (in Latin, *salutari convivio*) is not only more accurate, but provides us with a far richer metaphor to use than simply referring to "this meal." That in this saving banquet we are graciously endowed with Jesus' very own Spirit is a very powerful statement. "Fill us with his Spirit" does not carry the same full meaning found in the new translation of the Latin text. To ask God to take away "everything / that estranges us from one another" is a more powerful petition than simply saying, "May he take away all that divides us."

Obviously, the previous translation simplified the meaning and language of the Latin original. While the previous text may be easier to read, there is a greater richness and majesty captured by the new translation. It will take us a while to get used to praying it, but the effort will be worthwhile. There is a great deal of beauty and uplifting imagery captured in the new translation of this Eucharistic Prayer for Reconciliation II.

EUCHARISTIC PRAYERS FOR USE IN MASSES FOR VARIOUS NEEDS AND OCCASIONS

In the Decree issued by the Congregation for Divine Worship and the Discipline of the Sacraments (CDWDS) promulgating the use of the Eucharistic Prayers for Masses for Various Needs and Occasions, we are told that these prayers are based on what was formerly known as the "Swiss Synod Eucharistic Prayer."

While the original text of the Eucharistic Prayer for Various Needs and Occasions had been prepared on the occasion of the 1972 Synod of Bishops from the dioceses of Switzerland, the new composition was so well received that other language groups (German, French, and Italian) petitioned Rome for permission to translate the text into their own languages. Since this prayer was meant to be used in response to various circumstances, it provided additional variety to the Eucharistic Prayers currently in use at the time. Rome judged these needs to be sufficiently universal to approve the use of the prayer for the whole Church.

All four of these Eucharistic Prayers are short, similar in length to Eucharistic Prayer II. They have four special Prefaces: "The Church on the Path of Unity," "God Guides His Church along the Way of Salvation," "Jesus, the Way to the Father," and "Jesus, Who Went About Doing Good." In addition, the second half of the Eucharistic Prayer includes some variable intercessions corresponding to the themes already introduced in the

Preface. Otherwise, these four Eucharistic Prayers share the rest of their parts in common.

These four Eucharistic Prayers are easy to learn. They read very smoothly and have a good, poetic feeling to them. I believe that they will be very popular with our people. Increased use of these prayers is likely due to the fact that they are now published as part of the third edition of *The Roman Missal*. Formerly, they were published in a separate booklet and not included in the main body of *The Roman Missal*.

The new translation of these prayers is fairly close to the texts that we received permission to use in 1995. In the letter from the CDWDS, dated May 9, 1995, we read: "It has been decided that with this present letter permission is given to use this text only after the enclosed modifications have been made and may continue in use until such time as the new translation of the Roman Missal is presented for confirmation." Once we begin using the new translation, then we must cease using the old translation of the these Eucharistic Prayers.

I. The Church on the Path of Unity

Rubric number 1 says that "The following form of this Eucharistic Prayer is appropriately used with Mass formularies such as, For the Church, For the Pope, For the Bishop, For the Election of a Pope or a Bishop, For a Council or Synod, For Priests, For the Priest Himself, For Ministers of the Church, and For a Spiritual or Pastoral Gathering."

The previous translation of these prayers was made prior to 1995. The new norms for translating prayers, found in *Liturgiam authenticam*, came out on March 28, 2001. While the move to a more literal translation was already in evidence in the translation of these prayers, the full flowering of this movement had yet to take place until after the 2001 norms began to be used. Hence, there was a need to bring these prayers into accord with contemporary guidelines. Let's look at the Preface.

Previous Translation	New Translation
It is truly right to give you thanks, it is fitting that we sing of your glory, Father of infinite goodness. Through the gospel proclaimed by your Son you have brought together in a single Church people of every nation, culture, and tongue. Into it you breathe the power of your Spirit, that in every age your children may be gathered as one. Your Church bears steadfast witness to your love. It nourishes our hope for the coming of your Kingdom and it is a sure sign of the lasting covenant which you promised us in Jesus Christ our Lord.	It is truly right *and just* to give you thanks and *raise to you* a *hymn* of glory and *praise*, *O Lord*, Father of infinite goodness. For by the *word* of your Son's Gospel you have brought together one Church from every people, tongue, and nation, and, having *filled her with life* by the power of your Spirit, you *never cease* through her to gather the whole human race into one. Manifesting the *covenant* of your love, she *dispenses without ceasing* the *blessed* hope of your Kingdom and shines *bright* as the sign of your *faithfulness*, which in Christ Jesus our Lord you promised would last for eternity.

Once again, the phrasing in the new translation is different from that used in the prayers that we have gotten used to. The sentences are longer and more complex. However, they are more true to the phrasing and wording of the Latin original. I was surprised at how many words in Latin were never translated in the old 1995 text. The italicized words in the new translation above demonstrate this point. I had been hoping that a 1995 translation would have been more literal. As you can see, even in 1995 translators still felt a good deal of freedom to simplify the meaning of the Latin text, rather than to translate it more literally.

The new translation restores the rich metaphor found at the beginning of the Preface: "and raise to you a hymn of glory and praise." The sense of our prayers rising like incense before the throne of the Lord is based on the rich biblical image found in Psalm 141:2: "Let my prayers be counted as incense before you."

By referring to "the word of your Son's Gospel," you have a more engaging, fuller statement than merely saying "Through the gospel proclaimed by your Son." "Having filled her with life by the power of your Spirit" once again maintains biblical connections that are inadequately conveyed by "Into it you breathe the power of your Spirit." The use of inclusive language in the phrase "human race," rather than resorting to calling everyone "children," is also a welcome addition in the new translation. The Latin word being translated here is *hominem*, which means "mankind" or "human race." The Latin word for "children" is not used here.

The new translation restores the reference to "covenant of your love," thus conveying more accurately the affective content of this prayer. The word "covenant" has far richer connotations than merely talking about our steadfast "witness to your [God's] love." To dispense "without ceasing / the blessed hope of your [God's] Kingdom" is much more impressive and engaging than simply saying "nourishes our hope for the coming of your [God's] Kingdom."

There is also a strong, active sense of our ongoing efforts to minister to all the world by proclaiming the Good News that is captured by "dispense without ceasing the blessed hope of your Kingdom." To shine "brightly as the sign of your [God's] faithfulness" restores the beautiful image of the Church's faithful adherence to the covenant as a reflection (sign) of God's own faithfulness to this same covenant.

In short, there is a freshness to the vocabulary and the images used in this Preface that I believe will capture the imaginations and hearts of those who hear this prayer. Not only is the new translation more accurate, but it is also more engaging as a prayer.

To gain another perspective on this prayer, let's look at two paragraphs that are said after the Memorial Acclamation. Notice how the new translation adheres more closely to the word order of the Latin text, thus accounting for the different flow of the words in this part of the Eucharistic Prayer.

Previous Translation	New Translation
Renew by the light of the gospel the Church of N. (diocese/ place). Strengthen the bonds of unity between the faithful and their pastors, that together with N. our Pope, N. our bishop, and the whole college of bishops, your people may stand forth in a world torn by strife *and discord* as a sign of oneness and peace.	Lord, renew your Church (which is in N.) by the light of the Gospel. Strengthen the bond of unity between the faithful and the pastors *of your people,* together with N. our Pope, N. our Bishop, and the whole *Order* of Bishops, that in a world torn by strife your people may shine forth as a prophetic sign of unity and concord.
Be mindful of our brothers and sisters [N. and N.], who have fallen asleep in the peace of Christ, and all the dead, whose faith only you can know. Lead them to the fullness of the resurrection and gladden them with the *life* of your face.	Remember our brothers and sisters (N. and N.), who have fallen asleep in the peace of *your* Christ, and all the dead, whose faith you *alone* have known. *Admit* them to *rejoice* in the *light* of your face, and in the resurrection give them the fullness *of life.*

I italicized a few words in the previous translation that were added by ICEL, but that did not appear in the Latin text.

The italicized words in the new translation indicate all the words that either were not translated in the old text or that inadequately conveyed the meaning of the Latin text.

The new translation refers to the pastors "of your people" and the "Order of Bishops." The previous text did not mention "of your people" and chose the word "college" of Bishops. While we do refer to collegiality among the Bishops, it is more proper to speak of the Order of Bishops, since this is the word found in the Latin text, *ordine*.

The second paragraph refers to "your Christ." At first, it sounds strange to say "your" Christ, but this is what the Latin text does. Perhaps, the reason for adding the adjective "your" is to draw attention to the meaning of "Christ": the anointed one. The word *Christos* in Greek is the equivalent of the Hebrew word for "Messiah." Hence, there is a rich biblical connection to the name of Christ that is meant to be understood in this reference, a connection that eliminating "your" fails to make.

I believe the wording of "Admit them to rejoice in the light of your face" captures more dramatically the full meaning of the Latin text than the old translation's use of "Lead them" and "gladden them with the life of your face." When you pray for the deceased, you want them to be admitted to the heavenly Kingdom. Moreover, the word that the previous translation uses in referring to the "life of your [God's] face" really is not the meaning of the Latin text, which actually refers to the "light" of his face, *lumen vultus tui* in Latin.

The Latin text is more precise than the old translation indicates by using the words, "the fullness of the resurrection." The word "life" belongs with this reference to the Resurrection, not with the reference to God's face. Hence, the new translation, "and in the resurrection give them fullness of life," is really the more accurate translation of the Latin.

In conclusion, I found this particular prayer to be uplifting, hopeful, and filled with contemporary language that people will surely relate to. It reads quite easily, and I believe that most priests will like it. I encourage our priests to use this prayer when the occasion is suitable.

II. God Guides His Church along the Way of Salvation

Rubric number 1 says: "The following form of this Eucharistic Prayer is appropriately used with Mass formularies such as, For the Church, For Vocations to Holy Orders, For the Laity, For the Family, For Religious, For Vocations to Religious Life, For Charity, For Relatives and Friends, and For Giving Thanks to God."

Let's look at the Preface of this new Eucharistic Prayer:

Previous Translation	New Translation
It is truly right and just, our duty and our salvation, always and everywhere to give you thanks, Lord, holy Father, creator of the world and source of all life.	It is truly right and just, our duty and our salvation, always and everywhere to give you thanks, Lord, holy Father, creator of the world and source of all life.
You never abandon the creatures formed by your wisdom, but remain with us and work for our good even now. With mighty hand and outstretched arm you led your people, Israel, through the desert. By the power of the Holy Spirit you guide your pilgrim Church today as it journeys along the paths of time to the eternal joy of your kingdom, through Christ our Lord.	For you never *forsake the works* of your wisdom, but by *your providence* are even now at work in our midst. With mighty hand and outstretched arm you led your people Israel through the desert. *Now*, as your Church makes her pilgrim *journey* in the world, you *always accompany* her by the power of the Holy Spirit and *lead her* along the paths of time to the eternal joy of your Kingdom, through Christ our Lord.

The italicized words in the new translation indicate the number of words that were either not translated or mistranslated in the old text. The new translation literally translates the Latin text meaning "forsake the works of your wisdom." However, the previous translation substituted an explanation of this text as its translation: "You never abandon the creatures formed by your wisdom." While this is an interesting interpretation of the Latin text, it is not accurate. The Latin text refers to God never forsaking "the works of your [his] wisdom," not to never abandoning "the creatures formed by your [his] wisdom."

The previous translation completely skipped over the reference to God's "providence" in the second paragraph above. Yet God's providence is an important theological concept and reality on which we all depend. We need God to take care of us on our journey through life. I imagine the reference to God working "for our good even now" conveys this idea, but it still is not exactly what the Latin text says.

The adjective "pilgrim" really modifies the word "journey." It does not modify the word "Church," which is not used in this reference. The phrase to "always accompany" the Church on her pilgrim journey restores the image of God as our companion in our journey through life. The previous translation says "you guide your pilgrim Church today." By choosing to use the word "guide," they have obscured a powerful metaphor found in the Latin text. The sense of God being actively involved in our journey through life is enhanced when the new translation speaks of "lead[ing] her along the paths of time" rather than rely again on the verb "guide" to explain God's actions on our behalf. The image here is that of God taking us by the hand and leading us safely home to the eternal joy of his Kingdom.

This is a powerful prayer with strong images: "forsake the works of your wisdom," "mighty hand," "outstretched arm," "pilgrim journey," "paths of time," and "eternal joy." I found it to be very engaging, joyous, and hopeful. No wonder it was so well received at the 1972 Swiss Synod of Bishops.

Let's look at two paragraphs that are said after the Memorial Acclamation of this Eucharistic Prayer. The second paragraph is a repeat of a text which we have already discussed in talking about the first option in the Eucharistic Prayers for Use in Masses for Various Needs. I reprinted it here as an example of the use of "common texts" in these four Eucharistic Prayers.

Previous Translation	New Translation
Strengthen in unity those you have called to this table. Together with N. our Pope, N. our bishop, with all bishops, priests, and deacons, and all your *holy* people, may we follow your paths in faith and hope and radiate our joy and trust to all the world.	And so, having called us to your table, Lord, *confirm* us in unity, so that, together with N. our Pope and N. our Bishop, with all Bishops, Priests and Deacons, and your *entire* people, as we *walk your ways* with faith and hope, we may strive to bring joy and trust into the world.
Be mindful of our brothers and sisters [N. and N.], who have fallen asleep in the peace of Christ and all the dead whose faith only you can know. Lead them to the fullness of the resurrection and gladden them with the light of your face.	Remember our brothers and sisters (N. and N.), who have fallen asleep in the peace of your Christ, and all the dead, whose faith you alone have known. Admit them to rejoice in the light of your face, and in the resurrection give them the fullness of life.

While the two translations are very similar, there is greater accuracy in the last two lines of the first paragraph of the new translation in comparison to the previous translation. Where the previous translation refers to "radiate our joy and trust to all the world," the new translation more accurately says "may strive to bring joy and trust into the world." Of all the gifts needed in the world today, "joy and trust" need to be at the top of the list. To say "walk your ways with faith and hope" rather than "follow your paths in faith and hope" brings out more clearly the image of walking or putting into action the ways of Christ when he was on earth. There is an old saying today that "we should walk the talk."

This Eucharistic Prayer has phrases that will surely resonate with people: "confirm us in unity," "walk your ways," and "strive to bring joy and trust into the world." These are needs that we all have. God's people are the "leaven" mixed into society. Leaven makes the bread rise. Christians bring the world gifts of joy and trust that can enable the human race to reach new heights in its experience of communal living. I believe that people will be inspired by the sentiments captured in this prayer.

III. Jesus, the Way to the Father

Rubric number 1 says that "the following form of this Eucharistic Prayer is appropriately used with Mass formularies such as, For the Evangelization of Peoples, For Persecuted Christians, For the Nation or State, For Those in Public Office, For a Governing Assembly, At the Beginning of the Civil Year, and For the Progress of Peoples."

Let's look at the Preface of this Eucharistic Prayer. In the previous translation, I italicized all the words that were added to this Preface that are not found in the Latin text. In the new translation, I italicized words that were either not accurately translated or whose translation weakened the meaning of the Latin text.

While both translations are similar, the new translation does a better job at preserving the literal meaning of the Latin text. The new translation correctly translates the adjective "holy" modifying "Father." The previous translation turned this adjective into a genitive phrase: "of holiness." In the second paragraph,

Previous Translation	New Translation
It is truly right and just, our duty and our salvation always and everywhere to give you thanks, Father *of holiness*, Lord of heaven and earth, through our Lord *Jesus* Christ.	It is truly right and just, our duty and our salvation, always and everywhere to give you thanks, *holy* Father, Lord of heaven and earth, through Christ our Lord.
Through your *eternal* Word you created *all things* and govern *their course with infinite wisdom*. In the Word made flesh you have given us a mediator who has spoken your words to us and called us to follow him. He is the way that leads to you, the truth that sets us free, the life that makes our joy complete. Through your Son you gather into one family men and women created for the glory of your name, redeemed by the blood of the cross, and sealed with the *Holy* Spirit.	For by your Word you created *the world* and you govern *all things in harmony*. You gave us the *same* Word made flesh as Mediator, and he has spoken your words to us and called us to follow him. He is the way that leads us to you, the truth that sets us free, the life that fills us with *gladness*. Through your Son you gather men and women, whom you *made* for the glory of your name, into one family, redeemed by the Blood of his Cross and *signed* with the *seal* of the Spirit.

the Latin text (*mundum*) refers to "the world," which is correctly translated in the new text, whereas the old translation used the more generic term "all things."

The reference to "all things" really belongs in the next line, which the new translation correctly translates as "and you govern all things in harmony." The previous translation incorrectly talks about God "govern[ing] their course with infinite wisdom." There is a significant difference between the reference to harmony and the reference to wisdom. The implication of the Latin text is that if we followed the laws of God, if we let God govern according to his will, then the result would be greater harmony among all God's people. Speaking about "infinite wisdom" obscures the true meaning of the Latin text.

For the sake of variety in the translation of the Latin word *gaudio*, the new translation uses "gladness" rather than "joy." One of the goals in translating the Latin text was to capture more of the variety found in the vocabulary used in the Latin text. There are many ways to talk about joy. "Gladness" is a legitimate option for translating *gaudio*. There was some deliberation about how to translate the Latin verb *fecisti*, which is the second person singular of the perfect tense of the verb *facio*. The new translation chose to translate *fecisti* as "made" in the line "you made for the glory of your name." Some translators felt the biblical reference to God making man in his own image and likeness (Genesis 1:26) would be better captured by using "made" rather than "created."

The new translation restores the full meaning of the last line of the Latin text, which talks about God's family being "signed with the seal of the Spirit." The previous translation did not translate the Latin verb *signatos*, "signed," but instead changed the noun "seal" into the verb "seal." However, the Latin text clearly refers to the noun *sigillo* or "seal." The reason I referred to the actual words found in the Latin text above is to assure the reader that accuracy was paramount in creating the new translation of *The Roman Missal*.

This Preface is written in simple English, with words that most people will be familiar with. It is poetic and appeals to our deepest feelings: "the way that leads us to you, / the truth that sets us free, / the life that fills us with gladness." Isn't this really what all Christians need and desire? Don't we desire to live in a world governed by God's laws, a world where people live together in harmony? This Preface is one that will resonate well with the desires of most people.

Let's look at two paragraphs from after the Memorial Acclamation of the new translation of this Eucharistic Prayer:

Previous Translation	New Translation
Almighty Father, by our sharing in this mystery enliven us with your Spirit and conform us to the image of your Son. Strengthen the bonds of our communion with N. our pope, N. our bishop, with all bishops, priests, and deacons, and all your holy people.	By our *partaking* of this mystery, almighty Father, *give us life* through your Spirit, *grant* that we may be *conformed* to the image of your Son, and *confirm* us in the bond of communion, *together* with N. our Pope and N. our Bishop, with all other Bishops, with Priests and Deacons, and with your entire people.
Keep your Church *alert* in faith to the signs of the times and *eager to accept* the challenge of the gospel. Open our *hearts* to the needs of all *humanity*, so that sharing their grief and anguish, their joy and hope, we may faithfully bring them the good news of salvation and advance together on the way to your kingdom.	Grant that *all the faithful* of the Church, *looking into* the signs of the times by the *light* of faith, may *constantly devote themselves* to the *service* of the Gospel. Keep us *attentive to* the needs of all that, sharing their grief and *pain*, their joy and hope, we may faithfully bring them the good news of salvation and *go forward* with them along the way *of* your Kingdom.

There are quite a few places in the above prayers where the previous translation resorted to an interpretation rather than a strict, literal translation of the Latin text. The italicized words in the new translation indicate the places where the old translation was deficient in conveying the full meaning of the Latin text. Instead of saying "enliven us," the new translation asks God to "give us life." By spelling out the meaning of the verb "enliven" or *vivifica* in Latin, the new translation better conveys the full meaning of the Latin text.

There is a greater precision in the new translation. When you translate all the words, "Grant that all the faithful of the Church," you convey more fully the meaning of the Latin text, than by using the shorthand version found in the old translation: "Keep your Church." By translating *perscrutantes* as "looking into" the signs of the times, you have a more dynamic and accurate translation than the old translation's use of the phrase "alert in faith" to the signs of the times.

The previous translation departs from the literal meaning of the Latin text when it says "Open our hearts to the needs of all humanity." There is no mention of "hearts" or "humanity" in the Latin text. Literally, the Latin text means "open our eyes that we might recognize the needs of our brothers" (*fratrum* in Latin). The new translation unfortunately does not speak of opening our eyes, but instead chose to translate this line as "Keep us attentive." In the interest of using inclusive language, the new translation uses the pronoun "all" instead of the literal translation "brothers." I suspect they wanted to avoid saying "brothers and sisters," when the pronoun "all" would convey the same idea.

There is something more comforting to pray that we "go forward" with those suffering from grief and pain, or experiencing joy and hope. The sense of the members of the Church being mutual companions on our journey to the Kingdom is stronger in the new translation than in the old translation's reference: "to advance together." The art of translation is indeed difficult. Change one word, and a whole flood of connotations can suddenly be unleashed.

In this Eucharistic Prayer, you find some phrases and images that we have used in the previous prayers. So this prayer sounds a great deal like the other Eucharistic Prayers. This familiarity based on the repetition of key phrases should help this prayer's acceptance by the people and make the task of proclaiming this prayer easier for the Priest Celebrant.

IV. Jesus, Who Went About Doing Good

Rubric number 1 says: "The following form of this Eucharistic Prayer is appropriately used with Mass formularies such as, For Refugees and Exiles, In Time of Famine or For Those Suffering Hunger, For Our Oppressors, For Those Held in Captivity, For Those in Prison, For the Sick, For the Dying, For the Grace of a Happy Death, and In Any Need.

Let's look at the Preface of this Eucharistic Prayer:

Previous Translation	New Translation
It is truly right to give you thanks, it is fitting that we offer you *praise*, Father of mercy, faithful God.	It is truly right *and just*, our duty and our salvation, always and everywhere to give you thanks, Father of mercies *and* faithful God.
You sent Jesus Christ your Son among us as redeemer and Lord. He was *moved with compassion* for the poor and the powerless, for the sick and the sinner; he made himself neighbor to the oppressed. By his words and actions he proclaimed to the world	For you have given us Jesus Christ, your Son, as our Lord and Redeemer. He *always* showed *compassion* for *children* and for the poor, for the sick and for sinners, and he became a neighbor to the oppressed *and the afflicted*. By word and deed he announced to the world

that you care for us as a father *cares for his children.*	that you are our Father and that you care for all your sons and daughters.

In the previous translation, I italicized words that are not found in the Latin text, but were added for the sake of clarity. In the new translation, I italicized words that were omitted or mistranslated by the old translation. For example, the Latin text clearly refers to "children," *parvulos* in Latin, but the old translation hides this reference by referring to the "powerless."

The last line that ends the sentence spoken of above contains a beautiful metaphor presenting Jesus as "neighbor to the oppressed and afflicted" (in Latin, *oppressis et afflictis*). Unfortunately, the old translation only mentions the "oppressed." While this may sound like nitpicking, not translating all the words of the Latin text does have an impact on the effectiveness of this prayer to convey the full demands of Jesus' ministry to the needy.

This Preface expresses some strong sentiments that people want to hear: "He always showed compassion / for children and for the poor, / for the sick and for sinners, / and he became a neighbor / to the oppressed and the afflicted." These sentiments will certainly resonate with people today.

Let's look at two paragraphs after the Memorial Acclamation of this Eucharistic Prayer. In the previous translation, the italicized words either mistranslate the Latin text or are simply added to further explain the meaning of the text. In the new translation, the italicized words are all those left out or mistranslated in the previous translation.

While the two translations are similar, there are errors in the old translation. While the previous translation ("all those your Son has gained for you") is a biblical allusion, it is not what the Latin text literally says. The Latin text explicitly refers to the "entire people" (*omni populo* in Latin). Nowhere does the Latin

Previous Translation	New Translation
Lord, perfect your Church in faith and love together with N. our pope, N. our bishop, with all bishops, priests, and deacons, and all those *your Son has gained for you.*	Bring your Church, O Lord, to perfect faith and charity, together with N. our Pope and N. our Bishop, with all Bishops, Priests and Deacons, and the *entire people you have made your own.*
Open our eyes to the needs *of all*; inspire us with words and deeds to comfort those who labor and are burdened; *keep our service of others faithful* to the example and command of Christ. Let your Church be a living witness to truth and freedom, to justice and peace, that all people may be lifted up by the hope *of a world made new.*	Open our eyes to the needs of our *brothers and sisters*; inspire *in* us words and actions to comfort those who labor and are burdened. Make us serve them truly, after the example of Christ and at his command. And may your Church *stand* as a living witness to truth and freedom, to peace and justice, that all people may be raised up to a new hope.

text say "your Son has gained for you." However, a literal translation of the Latin text shows that this text refers to "the entire people" of your acquisition or purchase (*acquisitionis tuae* in Latin). If you have acquired or purchased something, you have made it your own. In this particular instance, neither translation does complete justice to the full meaning of the Latin text. However, I believe the new translation comes closer to doing so.

Rather than say "to the needs of all," the new translation is more specific: "to the needs of our brothers and sisters." Of course, people who favor inclusive language will like this translation. However, the word *fratrum* in Latin simply means "brothers." In the new translation, the translators tried to be sensitive to excluding people by using only male nouns when the text obviously is referring to all people.

The new translation corrects what can be interpreted as an error in emphasis in the old translation. The previous translation says "inspire us with words and deeds," obviously referring to God ministering to his people. However, the Latin text is very clear that this is not what is meant. "Inspire in us words and deeds" refers to our ministry to the needy, not Jesus' ministry to us. The Latin text uses the ablative *nobis* or "in us" and not the accusative *nos*. This is an easy mistake to make. However, the new translation is obviously more accurate than the previous translation.

As in the previous Eucharistic Prayer, we find phrases that were used in the other Eucharistic Prayers. We also find expressed very clearly the job description of a good Christian:

- Inspire in us words and actions
- Comfort those who labor and are burdened
- Make us serve them truly
- Follow the example of Christ
- Respond to Christ's command to serve
- Be a living witness to truth and freedom, to peace and justice
- Be raised up to new hope

I believe that the people who hear this prayer will be inspired by the sentiments expressed and find an easy connection between the themes found in this Eucharistic Prayer and other presidential prayers and quotes found in scripture. Therefore, this Eucharistic Prayer can be a wonderful complement to scripture readings and to a homily that refers to our ministry to the poor and oppressed.

QUESTIONS FOR CONTINUED REFLECTION

1. Do you approve of the new emphasis on accuracy that now guides the work of translators of the Latin text?

2. Were you surprised to learn of all the words in Latin that were either mistranslated or never translated into English?

3. Do you have much experience praying the Eucharistic Prayers for Reconciliation? Would you like to see them used more often?

4. Has the new translation been successful in restoring the obvious connections to biblical references as well as the images and metaphors contained in the Latin text?

5. What do you think of all the extra words added to the previous translation that were not found in the Latin text? Were these additions really necessary? Do you see these additions as an improvement over the more literal translation currently called for today?

6. Are you familiar with the Eucharistic Prayers for use in Masses for Various Needs? Have the priests in your parish made use of the previous translation of these prayers?

7. Which of the four Eucharistic Prayers for use in Masses for Various Needs most appeals to you?

   a) The Church on the Path of Unity
   b) God Guides His Church along the Way of Salvation
   c) Jesus, The Way to the Father
   d) Jesus, Who Went About Doing Good

8. Are there particular feasts or occasions when you would like your priest to consider using one of these Eucharistic Prayers?

Chapter 6
Proper of Saints

The next major section of *The Roman Missal* is the Proper of Saints. This particular section of *The Roman Missal* gives the celebrations of the saints assigned to the various months of the year, January through December. It identifies whether the particular celebration is a solemnity, a feast, an obligatory memorial, or an optional memorial. Consequently, it is important to know the differences between these four categories.

The four categories of Mass are explained in the decree *The Universal Norms on the Liturgical Year and the Calendar.* These are the pertinent passages from this important decree:

> 8. In the cycle of the year, as she celebrates the mystery of Christ, the Church also venerates with a particular love the Blessed Mother of God, Mary, and proposes to the devotion of the faithful the Memorials of the Martyrs and other Saints.

> 9. The Saints who have universal importance are celebrated in an obligatory way throughout the whole Church; other Saints are either inscribed in the calendar, but for optional celebration, or are left to be honored by a particular Church, or nation, or religious family.

> 10. Celebrations, according to the importance assigned to them, are hence distinguished one from another and termed: Solemnity, Feast, Memorial.

> 11. Solemnities are counted among the most important days, whose celebration begins with First Vespers

(Evening Prayer I) on the preceding day. Some Solemnities are also endowed with their own Vigil Mass, which is to be used on the evening of the preceding day, if an evening Mass is celebrated.

12. The celebration of the two greatest Solemnities, Easter and the Nativity, is extended over eight days. Each Octave is governed by its own rules.

13. Feasts are celebrated within the limits of the natural day; accordingly they have no First Vespers (Evening Prayer I), except in the case of Feasts of the Lord that fall on a Sunday in Ordinary Time or in Christmas Time and which replace the Sunday Office.

14. Memorials are either obligatory or optional; their observance is integrated into the celebration of the occurring weekday in accordance with the norms set forth in the *General Instruction of the Roman Missal* and the General Instruction of the Liturgy of the Hours.

Obligatory Memorials, which fall on weekdays of Lent may only be celebrated as Optional Memorials.

If several Optional Memorials are inscribed in the Calendar on the same day, only one may be celebrated, the others being omitted.

15. On Saturdays in Ordinary Time when no Obligatory Memorial occurs, an Optional Memorial of the Blessed Virgin Mary may be celebrated.

Selection of a Particular Mass to Celebrate. Sometimes people are confused as to why the priest decided to celebrate or not to celebrate a particular Mass on a particular day. The reason for his choice is dictated by the norms of the Roman calendar, which are quoted above.

On days that are optional memorials, the priest may prefer to celebrate the Mass of the day rather than the optional Mass of a saint about whom we know very little. On the Saturdays of Ordinary Time, as long as there is not a solemnity, feast, or obligatory memorial assigned, the priest may select a memorial in honor of Mary. There are many such Masses in the third edition of *The Roman Missal*, more than in the previous edition of *The Sacramentary*.

Why do we celebrate solemnities, feasts, and memorials of the saints? For years we have tried to get people to see the distinction between worshipping God and venerating (honoring) the saints. Worship belongs only to God. Honor is paid to people— the highest honor being paid to the Virgin Mary, Mother of God.

We honor the saints to remind us of the grace of God that triumphed in their lives, which we hope will triumph in our lives as well. We honor the saints because their lives reflect the Gospel values that Jesus came to teach us. We honor the saints because they are our heroes, whose courageous life sometimes led to their shedding their blood for the faith, much like Jesus himself.

Saints are a reflection of the image of God present in our world today. To imitate the saints is to choose the ways of the Lord. It is not simply a history lesson about one of the great exemplars of Christianity. If the Mass simply turns into a history lesson about a famous person, it is all too easy to say, "Good for them, but you don't expect me to live like that." To counter this temptation, the Church has consistently added new saints from every geographical region to reflect the universal calling we all have to live as one of God's holy, beloved people, his saints in the world (see Colossians 3:12).

MASSES FOR RECENTLY CANONIZED SAINTS

The third edition of *The Roman Missal* now includes Masses for new saints, for whom the previous edition of *The Sacramentary* did not have a Mass. This is due to the fact that the previous edition of *The Sacramentary* was published in 1970 and did not include all the new saints canonized under Pope John Paul II and Pope Benedict XVI. The third edition of *The Roman Missal* is consequently easier to use than the previous edition of *The Sacramentary* in that it contains Mass texts for the following recently canonized saints:

- January 6: Blessed André Bessette
- March 3: Saint Katharine Drexel
- May 10: Saint Damien de Veuster
- July 1: Blessed Junípero Serra
- July 9: Saints Augustine Zhao Rong and Companions
- July 14: Blessed Kateri Tekakwitha
- July 20: Saint Apollinaris
- July 24: Saint Sharbel Makhlūf
- August 9: Saint Teresa Benedicta of the Cross
- August 12: Saint Jane Frances de Chantal
- August 14: Saint Maximilian Kolbe
- September 20: Saints Andre Kim Tae-gŏn, Paul Chŏng Ha-sang and Companions
- September 23: Saint Pius of Pietrelcina
- September 28: Saints Lawrence Ruiz and Companions
- October 6: Blessed Marie Rose Durocher
- November 18: Saint Rose Philippine Duschesne
- November 23: Blessed Miguel Agustín Pro
- December 9: Saint Juan Diego Cuauhtlatoatzin

AN EXAMPLE OF A COLLECT FOR ONE OF OUR NEW SAINTS

Let's look at the Collect for the Mass in honor of Saint Maximilian Kolbe, priest and martyr, celebrated on August 14:

> O God, who filled the Priest and Martyr
>   Saint Maximilian Kolbe
> with a burning love for the Immaculate Virgin Mary
> and with zeal for souls and love of neighbor,
> graciously grant, through his intercession,
> that, striving for your glory by eagerly serving others,
> we may be conformed, even until death, to your Son.
> Who lives and reigns with you in the unity of the
>   Holy Spirit, one God, for ever and ever.

Notice how this new composition follows the traditions of the Roman prayer format for Collects. It begins by addressing God simply: "O God." It then tells you something about the saint being honored. This leads to an intercession ("graciously grant"—a traditional phrase seen many times before) and ends with a doxology praising God ("Who lives and reigns with you . . .").

Notice to the important use of adjectives, another hallmark of the Roman tradition. This prayer speaks of "burning love." What a powerful image set before us at the beginning of the prayer. Concise phrases, common to the Roman tradition, are also in evidence: "zeal for souls," "love of neighbor," "striving for your glory," "conformed . . . to your Son." There is a beauty and a poetic quality to this prayer. You can sense this in its conclusion, which asks God that "we may be conformed, even until death, to your Son." While this is a new Collect, it very much is written in a style consistent with the Roman tradition of prayer.

AN EXAMPLE OF A COLLECT FOR ONE OF OUR FAMOUS, OLDER SAINTS

Let's look at the new Collect from the Mass in honor of Saint Francis of Assisi, celebrated on October 4, and compare it to the old translation.

Previous Translation	New Translation
Father, you helped St. Francis to reflect the *image* of Christ through *a life of* poverty and humility. May we follow your Son by walking in the footsteps of Francis *of Assisi*, and by *imitating* his joyful love.	O God, by whose *gift* Saint Francis was *conformed* to Christ in poverty and humility, grant that, by walking in Francis' footsteps, we may follow your Son, and, through joyful charity, *come to be united with you.*

In the previous translation, I italicized all the words that were not found in the Latin text. In the new translation, I italicized all the words found in the Latin text that were not translated in the previous text. While the differences are fairly minor, they do give the prayer a different flavor. The first difference you notice is that the previous translation did not translate "by whose gift" (from the verb *tribuisti* in Latin). Seeing Saint Francis's ability to be conformed to Christ in poverty and humility as a gift or a blessing adds a dimension to the prayer not brought out in the old translation.

The previous translation talks about reflecting "the image" of Christ. Actually, the Latin text is more concise and simply speaks of being "conformed to Christ" (*Christo configurari* in Latin). The previous translation was preoccupied with explaining the Latin text, thus adding words that were not found in the Latin. In doing so, they failed to preserve the conciseness and simplicity of the original. Another example of this is when the old text speaks of "a *life* of poverty and humility." The word "life" is not found in the Latin text.

In the conclusion of the prayer, the old text fails to translate the complete meaning of the concluding words in Latin. The Latin text, *tibi coniungi*, talks about being "united with you [God]." This is an important theological concept to remind people of. When we act with joyful charity, we are following Christ and experiencing the joy of union with God. Union or communion with God is a major theme in our Roman prayer tradition.

THE MARIAN CYCLE OF MASSES

The third edition of *The Roman Missal* contains a more complete list of Marian Masses than the previous edition of *The Sacramentary*. You may be surprised to see how many Marian celebrations there are during the liturgical year:

- January 1: Solemnity of Mary, the Holy Mother of God

- February 11: Optional Memorial of Our Lady of Lourdes
- March 25: Solemnity of the Annunciation of the Lord
- May 31: Feast of the Visitation of the Blessed Virgin Mary

The Saturday following the Second Sunday after Pentecost: Optional Memorial of the Immaculate Heart of Mary. This Mass is found at the end of the month of May.

- July 16: Optional Memorial of Our Lady of Mount Carmel
- August 5: Optional Memorial of the Dedication of the Basilica of St. Mary Major
- August 15: Solemnity of the Assumption of the Blessed Virgin Mary
- August 22: Memorial of the Queenship of the Blessed Virgin Mary
- September 8: Feast of the Nativity of the Blessed Virgin Mary
- September 12: Optional Memorial of the Most Holy Name of Mary
- September 15: Memorial of Our Lady of Sorrows
- October 7: Memorial of Our Lady of the Rosary
- November 21: Memorial of the Presentation of the Blessed Virgin Mary
- December 8: Solemnity of the Immaculate Conception of the Blessed Virgin Mary

AN EXAMPLE OF A COLLECT FROM A MASS HONORING MARY

Let's compare the new translation of the Collect for the Solemnity of the Assumption of the Blessed Virgin Mary, August 15, with the text found in the previous edition of *The Sacramentary*.

Previous Translation	New Translation
Almighty *and* ever-living God, you raised the *sinless* Virgin Mary, mother of your Son, body and soul to the glory of heaven. May we *see heaven as our final goal* and come to share her glory.	Almighty ever-living God, who *assumed* the *Immaculate* Virgin Mary, the Mother of your Son, body and soul into heavenly glory, grant, we pray, that, *always attentive to the things that are above*, we may *merit* to be sharers of her glory.

Once again, the previous translation insists on adding words that are not found in the Latin and failing to translate important words that found in the Latin text. There is not "and" in the Latin text between the adjectives "Almighty ever-living." The previous text translates the Latin verb *assumpsisti* as "raised" rather than as "assumed." In doing so, it misses the opportunity to reaffirm the name of this solemnity.

The previous text explains the Latin rather than using a more literal translation. So the previous text translates the Latin *immaculatam* as "sinless" rather than as "Immaculate." The name given to the doctrine of Mary's conception in the womb of her mother is the "*Immaculate* Conception" (emphasis added). Moreover, one of the most popular hymns to sing on this day is "Immaculate Mary." The previous translation simply left out these important connections by using the word "sinless."

The Roman tradition is characterized by simplicity and directness in expression. Yet the old translation chose to use a genitive phrase, "of heaven," rather than the adjective "heavenly" when describing the glory Mary found in heaven. The Latin uses the adjective *caelestem* to modify "glory." It does not use the noun "heaven" or *coelum* in Latin. If you translate the Latin text more literally, you will also better exemplify the defining characteristics of the Roman tradition of prayer.

The previous translation explains the meaning of the Latin text when it says: "May we see heaven as our final goal." This is not what the Latin text says. The petition here is that we might be "always attentive to the things that are above" or *ad superna semper intenti* in Latin.

The previous translation ends abruptly, on a rather flat note, when it says "and come to share her glory." Actually, the ending of this Collect is more poetic and more precise. We pray that "we may *merit* to be *sharers* of her glory" (emphasis added) or *ipsius gloriae mereamur esse consortes*. The Latin text uses the verb *mereamur*, which means "may merit." It also uses the noun *consortes*, which means "sharers." When you summarize the meaning of the Latin, you are bound to lose some of the richness of meaning and poetic beauty found in the Latin text.

In addition to all the Masses listed above, there is an expanded list of thirteen Marian Masses in the Commons, which can be used on Saturdays in Ordinary Time. I will identify these Masses in the next chapter, since they are found in the Commons.

Next to Jesus himself, Mary is the highest example of sanctity in living that we have. God chose her to be the mother of his only-begotten Son, who was to be the Savior of the world. The way Mary lived each day of her life "proclaimed the greatness of God," as Mary says in the beautiful prayer, the Magnificat. On the cross Jesus gave Mary to the Church as our mother. In John 19:26–27, Jesus said to Mary: "Woman, here is your son." And to Saint John Jesus said: "Here is your mother." Saint John represents the whole Church in taking Mary into his home. We too take Mary into our lives, our homes each time we gather to celebrate one of her beautiful feasts throughout the liturgical year.

I think you will enjoy the Proper of Saints. There are many more Masses included in this section of the *Missal*. The new translation does a wonderful job of improving the previous translation in restoring the large number of metaphors, adjectives, and biblical references that sometimes were lost in the previous translation. The new compositions for the Masses of new saints beautifully capture highlights of each saint's life and reflect the values of the Roman tradition of prayer.

QUESTIONS FOR CONTINUED REFLECTION

1. Describe briefly the differences in the four categories of Masses found in *The Roman Missal*: solemnities, feasts, obligatory memorials, and optional memorials.

2. Why does a priest use a particular Mass on a particular day?

3. Why do we celebrate solemnities, feasts, and memorials of the saints?

4. Do you believe the addition of the Masses for newly canonized saints in *The Roman Missal* will be a positive contribution to your growth in the spiritual life? Why or why not?

5. Do you consider the new translation of the Masses honoring Saint Maximilian Kolbe and Saint Francis of Assisi to be improvements on the previous translation? Why or why not?

6. Were you surprised at the large number of Marian Masses celebrated throughout the liturgical year? Are there some Marian Masses that you do not know about?

7. Why do we have so many Masses honoring Mary?

8. Are you looking forward to praying the new texts and revised texts found in the new translation of *The Roman Missal* for the Proper of Saints?

Chapter 7
Commons

The following texts are found in the Commons:

Common of the Dedication of a Church
    On the Anniversary of the Dedication
      I. In the Church that Was Dedicated
      II. Outside the Church that Was Dedicated

Common of the Blessed Virgin Mary
      I. In Ordinary Time
      II. In Advent
      III. In Christmas Time
      IV. In Easter Time

Common of Martyrs
      I. Outside Easter Time
        A. For Several Martyrs
        B. For One Martyr

      II. During Easter Time
        A. For Several Martyrs
        B. For One Martyr

      III. For Missionary Martyrs
        A. For Several Missionary Martyrs
        B. For One Missionary Martyr

      IV. For a Virgin Martyr
      V. For a Holy Woman Martyr

Common of Pastors
    I. For a Pope or for a Bishop
    II. For a Bishop
    III. For Pastors
        A. For Several Pastors
        B. For One Pastor

    IV. For Founders of Churches
        A. For One Founder
        B. For Several Founders

    V. For Missionaries

Common of Doctors of the Church

Common of Virgins
    I. For Several Virgins
    II. For One Virgin

Common of Holy Men and Women
    I. For All Categories of Saints
        A. For Several Saints
        B. For One Saint

    II. For Monks and Religious
        A. For an Abbot
        B. For a Monk
        C. For a Nun
        D. For Religious

    III. For Those Who Practiced Works of Mercy
    IV. For Educators
    V. For Holy Women

Not every saint in *The Roman Missal* has a complete Mass (Collect, Prayer over the Offerings, Prayer after Communion). Some saints simply have a Collect, and still others make use of all the texts in the Commons, depending on the category into which they fall: martyr, pastor, doctor, virgin, monk or religious, one who practiced works of mercy, educator, or holy woman.

The use of commons texts recognizes the fact that there are many similarities in the lives of the saints. It is not necessary to create a complete set of Mass texts for every saint. If we did so, *The Roman Missal* would be an even bigger and heavier book than it already is. Rather, it is appropriate to make use of Masses found in the commons whenever the Missal directs you to do so.

All too often in many parishes, there is no celebration of the anniversary of the dedication of the parish church. Yet, this is a significant occasion in the history of a parish community. What meaning do you attach to the parish church? The Preface explains it in this fashion:

> For in this visible house that you have let us build
> and where you never cease to show favor
> to the family on pilgrimage to you in this place,
> you wonderfully manifest and accomplish
> the mystery of your communion with us.
>
> Here you build up for yourself the temple that we are
> and cause your Church, spread throughout the world,
> to grow ever more and more as the Lord's own Body,
> till she reaches her fullness in the vision of peace,
> the heavenly city of Jerusalem.

Celebrating the anniversary of the dedication of a parish church is a great way to renew our appreciation for the important events that take place in the church building and the many ways this building has shaped the faith of the people who worship there.

The Masses found in the Common of the Blessed Virgin Mary are often used on Saturdays, when there is no feast or mandatory memorial that we have to celebrate. There are Masses for every season of the year, including Ordinary Time. Where the former Missal had only three options for Ordinary Time, the third edition of *The Roman Missal* provides eight options for Ordinary Time.

It is well worth examining the new options found in the Common of the Blessed Virgin Mary for Ordinary Time. You will find some very moving, theologically rich, and poetically engaging prayers. For example, the Collect in the fifth optional Mass for Ordinary Time is truly a moving prayer:

> O God, who chose the Blessed Virgin Mary,
> foremost among the poor and humble,
> to be the Mother of the Savior,
> grant, we pray, that, following her example,
> we may offer you the homage of sincere faith
> and place in you all our hope of salvation.

Sometimes, we get into the habit of using the same Mass (usually, the first one in this section of the book) for Ordinary Time over and over again, rather than selecting one of the numerous options that can provide new inspiration for our prayer. I encourage celebrants and those who prepare the liturgy to make use of the variety of Masses found in the Common of the Blessed Virgin Mary.

In addition to these Masses, the priest may also use one of the Masses found in the *Collection of Masses of the Blessed Virgin Mary* that was published in 1988. While this book contains the previous Preface dialogue and the previous version of the Holy, Holy, Holy, the rest of the book can nonetheless be used until such time as it is revised or otherwise withdrawn from use. There are some wonderful Marian Masses in this *Collection*:

- The Visitation of the Blessed Virgin Mary
- Holy Mary, Mother of God
- The Blessed Virgin Mary at the Foot of the Cross I and II
- The Blessed Virgin Mary, Queen of Apostles
- The Blessed Virgin Mary, Seat of Wisdom
- The Blessed Virgin Mary, Image and Mother of the Church I, II, and III
- The Blessed Virgin Mary, Queen of All Creation
- The Blessed Virgin Mary, Mother of Good Counsel

- The Blessed Virgin Mary, Cause of Our Joy
- The Blessed Virgin Mary, Mother of Divine Hope
- The Blessed Virgin Mary, Health of the Sick
- The Blessed Virgin Mary, Queen of Peace

While *The Roman Missal* has increased the number of Marian Masses in the Missal, we also can continue to use our favorites from the *Collection of Masses of the Blessed Virgin Mary.*

The *General Introduction* to the *Collection*, 21, explains the source of the custom of celebrating these Masses and why the Vatican gave permission for their use:

The *Collection of Masses* is intended for:

> Marian Shrines where Masses of the Blessed Virgin
> Mary are celebrated frequently, in accord with the
> provisions indicated in nos. 29–33;

> Ecclesial communities that on Saturdays in Ordinary
> Time desire to celebrate a Mass of the Blessed Virgin,
> in accord with the provisions indicated in no. 34.

Where did the custom of celebrating a memorial Mass of Mary on Saturday come from, and why is it a good idea for congregations today to celebrate such a Mass? The *General Introduction,* 35–36, explains:

> The custom of dedicating Saturday to the Blessed
> Virgin Mary arose in Carolingian monasteries at the
> end of the eighth century and soon spread throughout
> Europe. The custom also was incorporated into litur-
> gical books of the particular Churches and became
> part of the heritage of the religious orders of evangeli-
> cal and apostolic life that were founded early in the
> thirteenth century.

> In the liturgical renewal following the Council of
> Trent, the custom of celebrating a memorial of the
> Blessed Virgin Mary on Saturday was incorporated
> into the *Missale Romanum.*

The liturgical reform initiated by the Second Vatican Council clarified the meaning of the memorial of the Blessed Virgin on Saturday and gave it new vigor by making possible a more frequent celebration of this memorial, increasing the number of formularies and biblical readings, and revising the euchological texts.

A number of ecclesial communities celebrate the memorial of the Blessed Virgin on Saturday as a kind of introduction to the Lord's Day. As they prepare to celebrate the weekly remembrance of the Lord's resurrection, these communities look with great reverence to the Blessed Virgin, who, alone of all his disciples, on that "great Sabbath" when Christ lay in the tomb, kept watch with full faith and hope and awaited his resurrection.

This "ancient and . . . as it were, humble memorial" of Mary recurring each week is in a certain way a reminder of the unfailing presence of the Blessed Virgin in the life of the Church.

And so, *The Roman Missal* continues this tradition by increasing the number of options found in the Common of the Blessed Virgin Mary.

The Common of Martyrs updates the translation of the Masses found in the previous Sacramentary. At the same time, these prayers are very helpful in focusing our attention on the inspiration that these martyrs provide for our spiritual lives. For example, the Collect from the first Mass Outside Easter Time, For Several Martyrs is truly remarkable:

> Grant a joyful outcome to our prayers, O Lord,
> so that we, who each year
> devoutly honor the day of the passion of the holy
>   Martyrs N. and N.,
> may also imitate the constancy of their faith.

Surely, this prayer inviting to imitate the constancy of the faith of the holy martyrs will address a common prayer among people of faith: patient perseverance.

The Collect for the third Mass "Outside Easter Time For Several Martyrs" is also a prayer that will resonate well with contemporary congregations:

> May the sight of the great number
> of your holy Martyrs gladden us, O Lord,
> making our faith stronger
> and bringing us consolation by the prayers of them all.

Despite the fact that this Collect comes from the Common section of the Missal, there is mention of specific prayer intentions and concrete spiritual goals for our lives that the faithful will appreciate when these Masses are used.

The Common of Pastors is also concrete in the petitions that are embodied in the collects of this section. For example, in the second Mass "For One Pastor," the wording of the Collect recalls our biblical traditions as it invites people to keep the faith taught by this saint:

> O God, light of the faithful and shepherd of souls,
> who set (the Bishop) blessed N. in the Church
> to feed your sheep by his words and form
>   them by his example,
> grant that through his intercession
> we may keep the faith he taught by his words
> and follow the way he showed by his example.

I am very impressed by the positive tone of these prayers and many ways in which they inspire our faith. I believe that people will enjoy hearing these prayers proclaimed at daily Mass.

The Common of Doctors (or teachers) of the Church offers two Masses for those teachers of the faith who have been honored with the title of "Doctor of the Church." In the Common of Virgins, you have one option for several virgins and

three options for one virgin. The Common of Holy Men and
Women has four options for several saints and two options for
one saint. There are five options for monks and religious. The
third edition of *The Roman Missal* adds a Mass "For a Nun" and,
in the section under "For Religious," provides special texts for a
woman religious. In general, the organization of these three sec-
tions (Common of Doctors, Common of Holy Men and
Women, and Common of Monks and Religious) is much clearer
in *The Roman Missal* and more attentive to the fact that often we
are praying for religious women.

The section after the Common of Monks and Religious
is the Mass "For Those Who Practiced Works of Mercy." In the
old Missal, this Mass was titled "For Those Who Work for the
Underprivileged." Notice how the Missal has returned to more
traditional, biblically oriented titles for the Masses. "Works of
Mercy" is certainly an improvement over the sociological term
"underprivileged." This biblical connection is also obvious in the
text of the Collect:

> O God, who have taught your Church
> to keep all the heavenly commandments
> by love of you as God and love of neighbor;
> grant that, practicing the works of charity
> after the example of blessed N.,
> we may be worthy to be numbered among the blessed
>   in your Kingdom.

By emphasizing the biblical basis of our faith and draw-
ing on themes and metaphors found in the apostolic preaching,
these prayers are certain to gain a warm reception from those
hearing them at Mass.

Where the previous Missal had a Mass "For Teachers,"
the revised Missal has broadened the title to "For Educators."
While the term "teacher" reminds us more of a classroom situation, the term "educator" has a broader connotation regarding
the place and the way in which someone teaches others. Since

these Masses will be used with saints who taught in a variety of ways and places, "Educators" is the better word to use here.

The final section of the Common is "For Holy Women." As in the previous Missal, two options are provided. I found the Collect in the second option to be inspiring in the way it combines biblical terminology and appropriate intercessions:

> Pour out upon us, Lord,
> the spirit of knowledge and love of you,
> with which you filled your handmaid blessed N.,
> so that, serving you sincerely in imitation of her,
> we may be pleasing to you
> by our faith and our works.

It is always helpful to look at all the options provided and choose the one that you believe will be the most spiritually nourishing for the people participating in this Mass.

In summary, the Common section of *The Roman Missal* contains some important Mass texts that are meant to be used with saints whose virtues and ministry are similar in character. Sometimes, the titles have been changed to use more traditional, biblical language. An easier division of the individual parts of each subsection of the Common should make finding a particular Mass less of a chore. Greater attention is paid to the needs of women religious. The choice of words is meant to restore more of the poetry and metaphors found in the Latin text.

QUESTIONS FOR CONTINUED REFLECTION

1. Why do we have a section of *The Roman Missal* with common Masses that may be used with a variety of saints and/or special occasions?

2. Why should we celebrate the anniversary of the dedication of our parish church? Why is this anniversary often forgotten? What can we do to make the anniversary of the dedication of our church a special day?

3. Does your community have the custom of celebrating a memorial Mass of Mary on Saturday, especially in Ordinary Time? Why is this a good idea? Where did this tradition come from?

4. What does your parish do to foster Marian devotion? Do you have any special shrines to Mary in your church? Are they in good repair? Are people aware of the particular devotion that inspired the creation of this shrine (for example, Our Lady of Guadalupe)?

5. Did you find any of the sample prayers quoted in this section inspiring? Why? What words, images, and metaphors captured your attention?

Chapter 8
Ritual Masses

The following texts are found in the Ritual Masses section of *The Roman Missal*:

    I. For the Conferral of the Sacraments of Christian Initiation
        1. For the Election or Enrollment of Names
        2. For the Celebration of the Scrutinies
            For the First Scrutiny
            For the Second Scrutiny
            For the Third Scrutiny
        3. For the Conferral of Baptism
        4. For the Conferral of Confirmation

    II. For the Conferral of the Anointing of the Sick

    III. For the Administering of Viaticum

    IV. For the Conferral of Holy Orders
        1. For the Ordination of a Bishop
            For the Ordination of One Bishop
            For the Ordination of Several Bishops
        2. For the Ordination of Priests
            For the Ordination of Several Priests
            For the Ordination of One Priest
        3. For the Ordination of Deacons
            For the Ordination of Several Deacons
            For the Ordination of One Deacon
        4. For the Ordination of Deacons and Priests in the Same Celebration

V. For the Celebration of Marriage

VI. For the Blessing of an Abbot or an Abbess
   1. For the Blessing of an Abbot
   2. For the Blessing of an Abbess

VII. For the Consecration of Virgins

VIII. For Religious Profession
   1. For First Religious Profession
   2. For Perpetual Profession
   3. For the Renewal of Vows

IX. For the Institution of Lectors and Acolytes

X. For the Dedication of a Church and an Altar
   1. For the Dedication of a Church
   2. For the Dedication of an Altar

In this section of *The Roman Missal*, Ritual Masses, we find Masses for the Sacraments of Initiation, the Anointing of the Sick, Viaticum, Holy Orders, Marriage, the blessing of an abbot or abbess, the consecration of virgins, religious profession, the institution of lectors and acolytes, and the dedication of a church and altar. Some of these liturgies are only presided over by a Bishop (subsections III, and V–IX).

The text for the Anointing of the Sick appears for the first time in *The Roman Missal*. The texts for the Anniversary of Marriage have been moved from this section on Ritual Masses to the next section: Masses and Prayers For Various Needs and Occasions. The texts "For the Blessing of an Abbot or an Abbess," "For the Institution of Lectors and Acolytes," and "For the Dedication of a Church and an Altar" appear for the first time in the revised Missal.

One of the reasons for including some texts in *The Roman Missal* that are celebrated only by the Bishop is that we do not have an up-to-date *Pontifical*, containing Masses and blessings celebrated by Bishops. Rather than wait to have a new

Pontifical issued, the decision was made to include these texts in *The Roman Missal* itself, making it easier for the Bishop to celebrate these special liturgies rather than having to bring a separate booklet with these prayers in it. It also gives us a chance to study the texts used in some very important liturgies: ordinations, the blessing of an abbot or an abbess, etc.

In the subsection "For the Conferral of the Sacraments of Christian Initiation," you have texts found originally in the *Rite of Christian Initiation of Adults.* The first option, "For the Election or Enrollment of Names," is used when the Rite of Election is celebrated within Mass, often with the Bishop as the celebrant. The recommended day is the First Sunday of Lent. The Masses for the three Scrutinies take place on the Third, Fourth, and Fifth Sundays of Lent. However, the Scrutinies themselves are found in the *Rite of Christian Initiation of Adults.*

The subsection "For the Conferral of Baptism" provides us with two sets of texts to be used when Baptism occurs at Mass. The rubrics note: "This Mass may be used with the color white or a festive color on days when Ritual Masses are permitted." Since the expectation is that most adults will be baptized at the Easter Vigil, these texts will most likely be used in the Baptism of infants at Mass.

If sickness or another serious reason prevents an adult from being baptized at the Vigil, then these texts are most suitable for the rites of initiation. Some of these texts make reference to the reception of Confirmation in parentheses ("and perfected with the seal of chrism"). If the person is not to be confirmed (e.g., a baptized infant), then this reference is dropped. When you are baptizing an adult, I recommend the second set of Mass texts in the section "For the Conferral of Baptism."

The Prayer over the Offerings in the second set of Mass texts for Baptism is a poetic masterpiece:

> Open the door to your supper, O Lord,
> for those who approach the bread that is prepared
> and the wine that has been mixed,

so that, celebrating the heavenly banquet with gladness,
we may be numbered as fellow citizens of the Saints
and members of your household.

In fact, all the prayers in these two Masses convey inspiring and theologically rich understandings of the Rites of Baptism and Confirmation, leading to First Holy Communion.

When the option to baptize candidates at Mass first came about, many parishes scheduled a regular Sunday Mass at which Baptisms would take place. However, due to the fact that many parishes had so many Sunday Baptisms, the added time needed to do the Baptisms properly led the demise of this option. Perhaps it is time to review this decision. Baptizing at Mass has the benefit of allowing the actual parish community to witness the initiation of its newest members and to rejoice with the proud parents and family of the newly baptized. Is there a place for Baptism at Mass in your parish community?

Confirmation usually is celebrated by a Bishop. In most dioceses, the candidates are junior high or high school students. If adults are to be confirmed, most dioceses offer special Masses for adult Confirmation. Except for the Confirmation of an RCIA candidate during the Easter Vigil, most people have not witnessed many Confirmations. Consequently, the Confirmation Mass is a very important moment in the life of a parish community. Not only do we pray for those who are receiving the Sacrament of Confirmation, but we also have the opportunity to ask God to renew the graces of this sacrament in our own lives.

There are three sets of texts in the section "For the Conferral of Confirmation." If you want to have a good review of the theology of Confirmation, then study these Mass texts. For example, in Option A, the Collect for the Conferral of Confirmation, we find a succinct understanding of Confirmation:

Fulfill for us your gracious promise, O Lord, we pray,
so that by his coming

the Holy Spirit may make us witnesses before the world
to the Gospel of our Lord Jesus Christ.

Some of the other Collects pray that we might become
"a perfect temple of his glory" or be raised to "the full stature of
Christ" so that our minds are enlightened and we walk in the
ways of truth and love.

In the subsection "For the Conferral of the Anointing of
the Sick," we are told to use the Mass for the Sick found in the
next chapter of the Missal, "Masses and Prayers for Various
Needs and Occasions." I was hoping that the Masses contained
in *Pastoral Care of the Sick: Rites of Anointing and Viaticum* would
be reprinted in the Missal. Unfortunately, this did not happen. I
hope either the Mass for the Sick or the Mass found in *Pastoral
Care of the Sick* will be used when communal Anointing of the
Sick takes place.

Pastoral Care of the Sick 132 states: "This rite may be used
to anoint a number of people within the same celebration. . . . It
is especially appropriate for large gatherings of a diocese, parish,
or society for the sick, or for pilgrimages." In order to participate
fully in the celebration, some of those who want to be anointed
may need to receive the Sacrament of Penance. This is why article 133 states: "The priest should ensure that the sick who wish
to celebrate the sacrament of penance have a convenient opportunity to do so before Mass."

When can you do the communal anointing of the sick at
Mass? *Pastoral Care of the Sick*, rubric number 134, says plainly:

> The ritual Mass for the anointing of the sick is not
> permitted during the Easter triduum, on the solemni-
> ties of Christmas, Epiphany, Ascension, Pentecost,
> Corpus Christi, or on a solemnity which is a holy day
> of obligation. On these occasions the texts and read-
> ings are taken from the Mass of the day. Although
> the ritual Mass is also excluded on the Sundays of
> Advent, Lent, and the Easter Season, on solemnities,

Ash Wednesday, and the weekdays of Holy Week,
one of the readings may be taken from the Scripture
texts indicated above, and the special form of the final
blessing may be used.

In the first instance (Easter Triduum, Christmas Time, Epiphany, Ascension, Pentecost, *Corpus Christi*, a holy day of obligation), the anointing of the sick is not permitted at Mass. In the second instance (Sundays of Advent, Lent, Easter Time, solemnities, Ash Wednesday, weekdays of Holy Week), the anointing is permitted, but the ritual Mass text "For the Sick" may not be used.

The texts listed under "For the Conferral of the Anointing of the Sick" are a collection of Solemn Blessings that can be used when the anointing takes place at Mass. They are similar to the blessings found in *Pastoral Care of the Sick*.

In the subsection "For the Administering of Viaticum," you will find a complete set of texts for Mass (Collect, Prayer over the Offerings, and Prayer after Communion). You will need these texts, since the section in *Pastoral Care of the Sick*, which speaks about Viaticum within Mass, does not provide these texts for the celebrant to use. However, the rest of the rite (Baptismal Profession of Faith, Litany, special introduction to Communion as Viaticum, Solemn Blessing, and Apostolic Pardon) is found in *Pastoral Care of the Sick*.

I have found Masses that I have celebrated for the Administration of Viaticum to be very moving experiences. The faith of the person to be anointed and their co-sufferers is truly amazing. I have done such Masses in the room of the sick person and in church, depending on the ability of the sick person to travel. If you are to do the Mass at home, it is best to work out the details ahead of time with a member of the family as to the needs you have for such a celebration (table, altar cloth, candles, wine, water, hosts, etc.)

The prayers in "For the Administering of Viaticum" set a hopeful, realistic tone for what is happening: A seriously ill person is preparing to die and meet the Lord. The Collect says it well:

O God, whose Son is for us the way, the truth
    and the life,
look lovingly upon your servant N.
and grant that, trusting in your promises
and strengthened by the Body of your Son,
he (she) may journey in peace to your Kingdom.

The Prayer over the Offerings makes reference to the Passion of Christ that "has unlocked the gates of paradise." It asks that God lead his servant to the gift of eternal life. The Prayer after Communion asks that God's servant "may safely reach your [God's] Kingdom of light and life." Consequently, there is a comforting, warm, and supportive tone set by the prayers of this beautiful Mass.

The subsection "For the Conferral of Holy Orders" contains the Ordination Rites for Bishops, priests, and deacons. It even has a combined rite for ordaining deacons and priests in the same celebration. The Mass texts are a rich source of our theology of Holy Orders. They are definitely worth studying in order to appreciate the significance of each of these rites.

You will find in the Prefaces to the Rites of Ordination a wonderful explanation of the theology of ministry contained in these Rites. The Prefaces for a Bishop, priest, or deacon have much in common. In fact, the same Preface is used for both Bishops and priests. In the ordination Preface, there is a good explanation of the difference between the common priesthood of all the baptized and priesthood of the ordained:

For by the anointing of the Holy Spirit
you made your Only Begotten Son
High Priest of the new and eternal covenant,
and by your wondrous design were pleased to decree
that his one Priesthood should continue in the Church.

For Christ not only adorns with a royal priesthood
the people he has made his own,
but with a brother's kindness he also chooses men

> to become sharers in his sacred ministry
> through the laying on of hands.

> They are to renew in his name
> the sacrifice of human redemption,
> to set before your children the paschal banquet,
> to lead your holy people in charity,
> to nourish them with the word
> and strengthen them with the Sacraments.

Of course, this prayer is not a complete theology of the office of Bishop, priest, or deacon. Important distinctions and responsibilities are found in other parts of the Rite.

In the Preface for the ordination of a deacon, the first two paragraphs quoted above are also used. However, paragraph three needed to be modified, since a deacon cannot consecrate the bread and wine (or celebrate Mass). This is reflected in a shortened version of the third paragraph above. The Preface for the ordination of a deacon says:

> He chooses them to lead your holy people in charity,
> to nourish them with the word
> and strengthen them with the Sacraments.

In other words, by using a common Preface for ordination, the Church draws attention to the common life and purpose that all the ordained ministers of the Church share. Obviously, their responsibilities and powers differ.

A Bishop is a member of the College of Bishops, charged with the authority to lead the Church. A priest shares in the priesthood of the Bishop, often representing the Bishop in ministering the sacraments to his people. The deacon has a strong commitment to sharing the Word of God and to the ministry of service. All three share a common awareness of their connectedness with Christ, of the ways they have come to share in Jesus' sacred ministry, and of their responsibilities to care for God's people.

In the subsection "For the Celebration of Marriage," you will find the new translation of the Mass texts for the Rite of Marriage. The rest of the texts for the Rite of Marriage are still being worked on. Hopefully, a new ritual book for marriage will be released in the near future, including the prayers found in *The Roman Missal* and updating the rest of the Marriage ceremony.

The Collects of the Masses "For the Celebration of Marriage" are very clear about the purpose of Marriage. There are two optional Collects for each of the three Masses found in the Missal. The Collect of Mass A states:

> Be attentive to our prayers, O Lord,
> and in your kindness uphold
> what you have established for the increase
>   of the human race,
> so that the union you have created
> may be kept safe by your assistance.

The themes of procreation and lifelong union are very much in evidence here. The Collect of Mass B states:

> O God, who consecrated the bond of Marriage
> by so great a mystery
> that in the wedding covenant you foreshadow
> the Sacrament of Christ and his Church,
> grant, we pray, to these your servants,
> that what they receive in faith
> they may live out in deeds.

This Collect reminds us of our biblical tradition and the famous text from Ephesians 5:32, which understands Marriage as a great mystery, a sacrament (sign) of Christ's lifelong commitment to his Church. The Collect of Mass C states:

> O God, who since the beginning of the world
> have blessed the increase of offspring,
> show favor to our supplications
> and pour forth the help of your blessing
> on these your servants (N. and N.),
> so that in the union of Marriage
> they may be bound together

in mutual affection,
in likeness of mind,
and in shared holiness.

This Collect again emphasizes the twin goals of marriage: procreation and union of mind and heart. While these Collects are not the only source of our understanding of marriage, they do deal very succinctly with the key ideas associated with the Catholic understanding of Marriage.

In the subsection "For the Blessing of an Abbot or an Abbess," you have one of those celebrations that most people never experience, unless you have a religious in the family and they invite you to participate in the installation ceremony of a new abbot or abbess. Once again, the Collects for these Masses provide a good idea of the office of abbot or abbess. It is interesting to see how close the wording is between these two Collects:

For the Blessing of an Abbot	For the Blessing of an Abbess
Grant, we pray, O Lord, to your servant N.,	Grant, we pray, O Lord, to your servant N.,
whom you have chosen as Abbot of this community of N.,	whom you have chosen as Abbess of this community of N.,
that by his deeds and his teaching	that by her deeds and her teaching
he may guide the hearts of his brothers	she may guide the hearts of her sisters
toward those things that are right,	toward those things that are right,
and so receive joyfully with them	and so receive joyfully with them
the recompense of an eternal reward	the recompense of an eternal reward
from you, the most loving Shepherd.	from you, the most loving Shepherd.

In these Masses, the Church not only points out the important duties and responsibilities of abbots and abbesses, but also reminds us how similar their roles are in their respective communities.

In the subsection "For the Consecration of Virgins," you find a liturgy that is being used more often today. While some people do not feel called to join a religious order, they do feel called to live a celibate life consecrated to God's service. After careful training and prayerful preparation, a Bishop may accept a woman into the ranks of consecrated virgins. The Collect explains this in a direct way:

> Grant, we pray, O Lord, to these your servants,
> in whom you have instilled a resolve to live in virginity,
> that the work you have begun in them
> may be brought to fulfillment
> and that they may be found worthy
> to complete what they now begin,
> so as to bring you a full and perfect offering.

The order of consecrated virgins is an ancient part of Church life. The Fathers of the Church speak of consecrated virgins who have dedicated themselves "in perpetuity to divine worship and the service of humanity." By restoring this order in this day and age, the Church gives prophetic witness to our belief that there is more to life than simply the cares of the flesh. Dedication to a life of prayer and service is indeed an important witness needed in the world today.

The subsection "For Religious Profession" is again a set of Masses that, if you do not have a religious in your life or contact with a religious community, you may never witness. Yet the first religious profession, the perpetual profession, and the renewal of vows, usually on an anniversary or on the founder's day, are impressive, joyful Masses, where the gift of one's life to God is clearly recognized and valued. In the Collect "For First Religious Profession," we read:

> O Lord, who have inspired these our brothers (sisters)
> with the resolve to follow Christ more closely,
> grant them, we pray,
> a blessed end to the journey they now begin,
> so that they may be found worthy to offer you
> a perfect gift of loving service.

One of the hallmarks of the Roman liturgy is that its prayers are readily understandable, succinct, and poetic. You find all that in evidence here.

In the Collect "For Perpetual Profession," you have a prayer for a religious who has proven over the years to have the ability to serve God, to live in community, to observe the evangelical counsels (poverty, chastity, and obedience), and to live a holy life. Hence, the Collect "For Perpetual Profession" goes beyond the more generic goals found in the Collect "For First Religious Profession." This Collect states:

> O God, who willed that the grace of Baptism
> should flourish in these your servants,
> so that they might strive to follow more closely
> in the footsteps of your Son,
> grant, we pray,
> that, constantly seeking evangelical perfection,
> they may add to the holiness of your Church
> and increase her apostolic zeal.

Of course, these Collects need to be read in the larger context of all the Mass texts (Prayer over the Offerings, Preface, Special Intercessions added to the Eucharistic Prayer, Prayer after Communion, and Solemn Blessing) in order to gain a fuller appreciation of the important commitment that we are celebrating in this Mass.

In the subsection "For the Institution of Lectors and Acolytes," you have the rite for the installation of a layman as a lector or an acolyte. Since at present only men can be installed in these ministries, most Bishops have chosen not to celebrate this rite, in deference to the fact that they would have to exclude women as candidates.

Since this rite is based on the rite used for the minor orders of lector and acolyte, there is a worry that if we began to install women in these ministries, then we may inadvertently give encouragement to women to pursue ordination, which also is forbidden to women. After all, the old minor orders were viewed as preludes to major orders. Seminarians who received the old minor orders were on a track that led to ordained ministry. Yet the fact that we no longer call these minor orders, but ministries, has led some to argue that both men and women should be eligible for installation into these ministries. There has been no movement on resolving this question for many years.

In the subsection "For the Dedication of a Church and an Altar," there are two beautiful Masses, both of which are rich sources of our theology of Church and altar. These two services can be very moving and inspiring. Anyone who has witnessed the dedication of a church remarks how like a sacred person that church is treated. Anyone who has witnessed the anointing of the altar with oil cannot help but make parallels to the anointing of Christ's body after his Death on the Cross.

In the Preface of the Mass "For the Dedication of a Church," you have a beautiful and inspiring explanation of the purpose of a church:

> For you have made the whole world a temple of your glory,
> that your name might everywhere be extolled,
> yet you allow us to consecrate to you
> apt places for the divine mysteries.
>
> And so, we dedicate joyfully to your majesty
> this house of prayer, built by human labor.
>
> Here is foreshadowed the mystery of the true Temple,
> here is prefigured the heavenly Jerusalem.

For you made the Body of your Son, born of the tender
    Virgin,
the Temple consecrated to you,
in which the fullness of the Godhead might dwell.

You also established the Church as a holy city,
built upon the foundation of the Apostles,
with Christ Jesus himself the chief cornerstone:
a city to be built of chosen stones,
given life by the Spirit and bonded by charity,
where for endless ages you will be all in all
and the light of Christ will shine undimmed for ever.

Note the use of strong biblical images: temple of your
glory, heavenly Jerusalem, fullness of the Godhead, a holy city,
the chief cornerstone, chosen stones given life by the Spirit and
bonded by charity. This prayer is indeed a great masterpiece,
preserving major themes from our Catholic tradition.

In the Preface of the Mass "For the Dedication of an
Altar," you have another powerful explanation of the deep significance of the altar in the church:

Having become both the true Priest and the true
    oblation,
he has taught us to celebrate for ever
the memorial of the Sacrifice
that he himself offered to you on the altar of the cross.

Therefore, Lord, your people have raised this altar,
which we dedicate to you with joyful praise.

Truly this is an exalted place,
where the sacrifice of Christ is ever offered in mystery,
where perfect praise is rendered to you
and redemption flows forth for us.

Here is prepared the table of the Lord,
where your children, fed by the Body of Christ,
are gathered into the one, the holy Church.

Here the faithful drink of your Spirit
from the streams that flow from Christ, the spiritual
   rock,
through whom they, too, become a holy oblation,
   a living altar.

The altar is a symbol of Christ himself, offered on the altar of the Cross. It is a sacred object, upon which the sacred mysteries are celebrated, perfect praise is given to God, and redemption flows out to God's people. It is the table of the Lord, recalling the table at which Jesus celebrated his Last Supper, the place where God continues to feed us with his Body and Blood. It is a place where our oneness as a Church is most in evidence. It reminds us of the way the Spirit has flowed into our life from Christ, transforming us and enabling us to see ourselves as holy offerings (oblations), living altars giving praise and glory to God.

In summary, the Ritual Masses contain some of the most important Masses we celebrate throughout the year: Mass for Christian Initiation, Anointing of the Sick, administering Viaticum, Holy Orders, Marriage, blessing an abbot or abbess, consecrating a virgin, religious profession, institution of lectors and acolytes, and the dedication of a church and an altar. While these are important celebrations, many of them are used occasionally. Consequently, this section of the Missal contains celebrations that people may not be too familiar with. If that is the case, then some catechesis may be necessary before a particular celebration (e.g., consecrating a virgin, religious profession, dedication of a church and an altar) in order for it to have the greatest impact upon the participants.

QUESTIONS FOR CONTINUED REFLECTION

1. How many of the Ritual Masses are you familiar with or have participated in? Which ones are new to you? Which ones would you like to learn more about? Why?

2. How successful is the Rite of Christian Initiation of Adults (RCIA) in your parish? Do you celebrate the Rite of Sending a person to the Bishop for the Rite of Election at the beginning of Lent? Do you understand what a scrutiny is and why we use these prayers on the second, third, and fourth Sundays of Lent?

3. Have you participated in a Baptism at Mass? What was your reaction to witnessing the Baptism? Did it stir up memories of your own, your children's, or your friends' Baptisms? Did the families having their children baptized experience the support of the parish community in a more powerful way than they if they simply celebrated Baptism in a ceremony without Mass? Does your parish favor Baptism at Mass? Why or why not?

4. When was the last time you witnessed a Confirmation? Does it make a difference to you that you were confirmed by a Bishop? What does the Bishop's participation in Confirmation add to the liturgy? What is the meaning of Confirmation, based on your examination of the prayers for Confirmation Masses?

5. Have you ever participated in a communal Anointing of the Sick at Mass? What was the reaction of the sick persons to celebrating the anointing at Mass? What was the reaction of the congregation? Did the congregation see this as an opportunity to reach out to the sick, to comfort and support them? What is the most memorable part of the Mass for the communal Anointing of the Sick?

6. Have you ever participated in the administration of Viaticum? Did it take place in a hospital, nursing home, private home, chapel, or church? Was Mass celebrated along with Viaticum? What impact did Mass with the

administration of Viaticum have on the sick person and the family and friends gathered around them?

7. What do the three Rites of Ordination have in common? Despite the difference in authority and responsibility, what do you see as the key responsibilities all ordained ministers have in common? Have you ever witnessed an ordination? What impact did the Rite of Ordination have upon the candidate, his immediate family, the parish, and the community at large?

8. When was the last time you participated in a wedding Mass? What is the basic theology of Marriage according to the Catholic Church? Do your wedding prayers do a good job reflecting this basic theology? What is the typical experience of a wedding in your parish like? What is necessary in order for the wedding Mass to be a positive experience for all involved?

9. What do you see as the role of an abbot or an abbess? Were you surprised to learn that the Collects said in their respective Masses were almost identical? Is this important to you?

10. What is the difference between a Mass for the consecration of a virgin and a religious profession? Why would someone choose to live a celibate life dedicated to prayer and service without joining a religious order? What benefits do you see in being part of a religious order? Have you ever seen the consecration of a virgin or a religious profession?

11. Would you like to see the Rite for the Institution of a Lector or Acolyte celebrated in your diocese? Is it celebrated in your diocese? Does the exclusion of women candidates from this rite trouble you? Why or why not?

12. Have you ever witnessed the dedication of a church or an altar? What impressed you the most? Were there any surprises in the Prefaces when they described the purposes of a church and an altar? Were there new images that you can remember from these Prefaces?

Chapter 9
Masses and Prayers for Various Needs and Occasions

Part I. For Holy Church

The section on Masses and Prayers for Various Needs and Occasions contains an interesting set of Masses that at times are forgotten and seldom used. Whether it is the large number (forty-nine) of Masses in this section of the Missal or simply the lack of familiarity with some of these Masses, many priests choose to use one of the Sunday Masses on a day when there is no obligatory memorial, feast, or solemnity rather than investigate other options in the Missal.

One way to avoid falling into the rut of constantly using the Sunday Mass texts is to consult the *Ordo*—the small book that contains recommendations for every day of the year. Often, the *Ordo* points out that the Scripture readings of the day work well with one of the Masses and Prayers for Various Needs and Occasions. In addition, when a special Mass is celebrated for school children, sometimes a knowledgeable teacher recommends the use of a Mass from this section of the Missal. Finally, the occasion itself (for example, a wedding anniversary) causes the priest to consult this section of the Missal in order to find appropriate prayers for the particular occasion that he is asked to celebrate.

Let us review the forty-nine Masses contained in Masses and Prayers for Various Needs and Occasions:

I. For Holy Church
   1. For the Church
   2. For the Pope
   3. For the Bishop
   4. For the Election of a Pope or a Bishop
   5. For a Council or a Synod
   6. For Priests
   7. For the Priest Himself
   8. For Ministers of the Church
   9. For Vocations to Holy Orders
   10. For the Laity
   11. On the Anniversaries of Marriage
   12. For the Family
   13. For Religious
   14. For Vocations to Religious Life
   15. For Promoting Harmony
   16. For Reconciliation
   17. For the Unity of Christians
   18. For the Evangelization of Peoples
   19. For Persecuted Christians
   20. For a Spiritual or Pastoral Gathering

II. For Civil Needs
   21. For the Nation or State
   22. For Those in Public Office
   23. For a Governing Assembly
   24. For the Head of State or Ruler
   25. At the Beginning of the Civil Year
   26. For the Sanctification of Human Labor
   27. At Seedtime
   28. After the Harvest

One way to ensure that you make better use of the Masses in this section of the Missal is to invite the liturgy committee to develop a plan for the liturgical year that emphasizes key celebrations and relates the liturgy to events taking place in the larger world. For example, when would it be appropriate to celebrate a Mass using the texts from the Masses "For the Church"? In making this decision, it is necessary to consult the scripture readings for daily Mass. For example, if the Gospel of the day contains the famous quote from Matthew 16:18 ("I tell you, you are Peter, and upon this rock I will build my church, and the gates of Hades will not prevail against it"), then using the Mass "For the Church" is fairly obvious. There are five Masses "For the Church" from which to choose. If you chose Option A, the Collect would complement well the Gospel from Matthew:

> O God, who in your wonderful providence
> decreed that Christ's kingdom
> should be extended throughout the earth
> and that all should become partakers of his
>   saving redemption,
> grant, we pray, that your Church
> may be the universal sacrament of salvation
> and that Christ may be revealed to all
> as the hope of the nations and their Savior.

Notice the poetry and rich theology embodied in this prayer, which is easily understood and proclaimed. Surely, this prayer needs to be used more often.

The fifth option in the Masses "For the Church" is a Mass "For the Particular Church." By "particular" Church, they mean the diocesan Church. Practically every diocese has a diocesan collection for the work of the diocesan Church, its agencies, and its offices. Perhaps, during the week before or after this collection is taken up, a prayer reminding people of the important work of the diocesan Church would be appropriate.

Sometimes, we are so parish-oriented that we lose sight of the important works of the local Bishop, the diocese, its agencies, and its offices. The Collect from the fifth option "For the Church" reminds people of the larger Church of which the parish is a part.

> O God, who in each pilgrim Church
>   throughout the world
> make visible the one, holy, catholic
>   and apostolic Church,

graciously grant
that your faithful may be so united to their shepherd
and gathered together in the Holy Spirit
through the Gospel and the Eucharist,
as to worthily embody the universality of your people
and become a sign and instrument in the world of the
   presence of Christ.

It is good to be reminded of the goals we share as a diocese in carrying on the work of Jesus in our local Church.

The Masses "For the Pope" and "For the Bishop" have important subtitles that indicate when these Masses are to be used: "For the Pope: Especially on the Anniversary of Election" and "For the Bishop: Especially on the Anniversary of Ordination." Pope Benedict XVI's anniversary of election is April 19. You can find your Bishop's anniversary of ordination by consulting the diocesan Web site or by looking up the name of your diocese in the *Official Catholic Directory*, a large book containing all the dioceses of the United States of America, listing the names of all the Bishops, priests, and religious working in our country. We should pray for the Pope and our diocesan Bishop in a special way on their anniversaries.

After a Pope or Bishop dies and before a new Pope is elected or a new Bishop is appointed, there is a beautiful Mass "For the Election of a Pope or a Bishop" that many people forget to use during the time before the new Pope or Bishop takes office. Yet these Mass prayers are truly outstanding. For example, the Prayer after Communion states:

As we have been renewed, O Lord,
with the supreme Sacrament of salvation,
the Body and Blood of your Only Begotten Son,
may the wondrous grace of your majesty
gladden us with the gift of a shepherd
who will instruct your people by his virtues
and imbue the minds of the faithful with the truth of
   the Gospel.

Notice the positive, hopeful, joyful tone of this prayer. Making use of this prayer prior to the new Pope or Bishop taking office can assist people in developing a welcoming spirit to accept the leadership of their new Pope or Bishop.

Every few years, there is a Synod of Bishops, a representative sampling of the world's Catholic Bishops, that usually takes place in Rome. While an ecumenical council is a rarity, we have had 25 Synods of Bishops since the conclusion of Vatican Council II (1965). Pope Paul VI established the Synod of Bishops when he issued the *motu proprio, Apostolica sollicitudo*, of September 15, 1965. It would be appropriate to make use of the Mass "For a Council or Synod" sometime before the next Synod this fall, 2011.

If a parish is having a "vocation week" in which one of the topics is the vocation to the priesthood, it is appropriate to use the first option in "For Priests." In the Mass "For the Priest Himself, Especially for a Priest with the care of souls" you have another option that the priest might choose, if he has been talking about vocations to the priesthood. Moreover, there are times when the parish may want to pray for its pastor—for example, when a pastor has recently been appointed or has had a second term of office granted to him. There are two options under "For the Priest Himself" whose prayers remind us of the important responsibilities and ministries entrusted to a priest. I recommend that we find a suitable day to use one of these Masses.

Of course, every priest celebrates his anniversary of ordination. Some do this privately, while others invite their classmates to a special concelebrated Mass followed by a dinner in the parish hall. Regardless of how a priest celebrates his anniversary, it is a significant occasion, not just to the priest himself, but also to the people who benefit from his priestly ministry. The prayers contain important reminders of the ideal a priest is striving for. For example, the Collect says:

> Holy Father, who, by no merit of my own, chose me
> for communion with the eternal priesthood
>   of your Christ

and for the ministry of your Church,
grant that I may be an ardent yet gentle preacher
    of the Gospel
and a faithful steward of your mysteries.

Using the Mass "For a Priest on the Anniversary of his Ordination" can benefit both the priest and his people, who want to support their priest in living up to the challenges of priestly life and ministry.

The Mass "For Ministers of the Church" is most appropriate to use on an occasion celebrating the work of ministers in general (priests, deacons, lay ministers) and for permanent deacons. The Collect prays to God that "they may be effective in action, gentle in ministry, and constant in prayer." Certainly, this prayer fits the general work of ministers in the Church.

I am sure our permanent deacons will identify with the ministries referred to at the end of the Prayer after Communion:

Grant, O Lord, to your servants,
whom you have replenished with heavenly
    food and drink,
that, for the sake of your glory and the salvation
    of believers,
they may be found faithful as ministers of the Gospel,
of the Sacraments and of charity.

Often, permanent deacons speak of themselves as "ministers of the Gospel, / of the Sacraments and of charity." If you have a candidate preparing for ordination as a deacon, this would be an appropriate Mass to use either before or after his ordination.

There are some very good Masses "For Vocations to Holy Orders" and "For the Laity" are also found in this section of the Missal. Since the Mass "For the Laity" is placed right after the Mass "For Vocations to Holy Orders," we are reminded that we also need to pray for those who are called to live in the midst of the world and its affairs, for they too play an important role in the building up of God's Kingdom on earth.

There are three Masses "On the Anniversaries of Marriage": "On Any Anniversary," "On the Twenty-Fifth Anniversary," and "On the Fiftieth Anniversary." The prayers are quite appropriate for the occasion, expressing thoughts that are often in the hearts of those praying for a married couple on their anniversary. For example, the Prayer after Communion in the Mass "On Any Anniversary" expresses well the sentiments of the gathered assembly:

> Open wide in joy and love, O Lord,
> the hearts of these your servants,
> who have been refreshed with food and
>   drink from on high,
> that their home may be a place of decency and peace
> and welcome everyone with love.

The prayers in the other Masses are also good in expressing the joy that is in our hearts, our gratitude for the past, and our hopes for the future of the couple celebrating their twenty-fifth or fiftieth anniversary.

As you might expect after a group of Masses celebrating wedding anniversaries, the next Mass is a Mass "For the Family." If we going to address the need for obedience and discipline, sharing and caring in family life, then the Mass "For the Family" is an ideal complement to these themes. The Collect is a masterpiece, rich in biblical imagery and explicit in the challenges to family life today:

> O God, in whose eternal design
> family life has its firm foundation,
> look with compassion on the prayers of your servants
> and grant that, following the example
> of the Holy Family of your Only Begotten Son
> in practicing the virtues of family life
>   and in the bonds of charity,
> we may, in the joy of your house,
> delight one day in eternal rewards.

Surely, there are occasions during the week when the scriptures of the day or a special event like a retreat for married couples (for example, a marriage encounter) are appropriate occasions to make use of this beautiful Mass "For the Family."

Having addressed the needs of the clergy and the laity, we now turn to the needs of religious. There are two options in the Masses "For Religious." The second option is "On the Twenty-Fifth or Fiftieth Anniversary of Religious Profession." Those parishes that are blessed with the presence of a religious (priest, brother, sister) working in their parish, should take note of the anniversaries of these dedicated servants of the community, especially on occasions such as a twenty-fifth or fiftieth anniversary. The Collect of the anniversary Mass for religious is quite beautiful:

> O Lord, faithful God,
> grant, we pray, that we may give you thanks
> for your kindness towards our brother (sister) N.,
> who today is eager to renew the gift received from you;
> strengthen in him (her) a spirit of perfect charity,
> so that each day he (she) may more fervently serve
>   your glory
> and the work of your salvation.

Even if the religious has already celebrated the renewal of vows at a Mass in the motherhouse or headquarters of the community, a local celebration is also appropriate, especially with people unable to attend the celebration at the motherhouse or headquarters.

Since we are talking about religious life in the Masses "For Religious," it is appropriate to provide a Mass "For Vocations to Religious Life." While we certainly make intercession for vocations to the priesthood, we should not forget the tremendous good that is being done by so many dedicated men and women religious. Religious orders, similar to the diocesan clergy, have also seen a downturn in numbers of vocations. If you have a missionary coming to preach at all the Masses on Sunday, perhaps the week before or after would be a good time to celebrate a Mass "For Vocations to Religious Life."

The next three Masses are "theme" Masses: "For Promoting Harmony," "For Reconciliation," and "For the Unity of Christians." With the ongoing violence on the streets and even in our homes, the use of a Mass "For Promoting Harmony" can help to provide hope and comfort to a people suffering from the destructive impact of violence today. So too when relationships among peoples are strained and call for a special penitential time to pray for healing and forgiveness, a Mass "For Reconciliation could be a big help. Of course, the Eucharistic Prayers for Reconciliation may also be used to further complement the themes found in the Mass prayers.

The theme of the unity of Christians is so important that the Missal has three Masses on this theme, along with a special Preface. Of course, every January we have the Week of Prayer for Christian Unity. Most dioceses and/or clusters of parishes conduct ecumenical services, especially near Thanksgiving. These would certainly be obvious times to use one of the Masses "For the Unity of Christians." The special Preface of the Mass for unity captures well the sentiments of these Masses:

> For through him you brought us
> to the knowledge of your truth,
> so that by the bond of one faith and one Baptism
> we might become his Body.
>
> Through him you poured out
> your Holy Spirit among all the nations,
> so that in a wondrous manner
> he might prompt and engender unity
> in the diversity of your gifts,
> dwelling within your adopted children
> and filling and ruling the whole Church.

Interest in praying for Christian unity comes and goes, but the need for Christians to work together in carrying out the ministry of Jesus in the world is constant and growing more important each day. Celebrating the Mass "For the Unity of Christians" is a good way to raise this consciousness periodically among our people.

The next three Masses are for special groups of people. First, we have two Masses "For the Evangelization of Peoples." The Church considers this such an important topic that the rubrics say: "This Mass may be used even on Sundays in Ordinary Time, whenever there are special celebrations for the work of the missions, provided it does not occur on a Sunday of Advent, Lent or Easter, or on any Solemnity." Our current Holy Father, Pope Benedict XVI, has been very articulate about the need for a new wave of evangelization of God's people. Consequently, this topic comes up during the year with great frequency.

When the scriptures discuss the disciples going forth to preach the Gospel, when the parish has its "Mission Sunday," when it is the Week of Prayer for Christian Unity, or when the Bishop or Pope addresses the need for evangelization, these are all times when it would be appropriate to celebrate one of the two Masses "For the Evangelization of Peoples." These Masses may be celebrated either during the week or, if we are in Ordinary Time, on Sunday. I encourage you to make good use of one of these two Masses. People will enjoy hearing these prayers.

Second, we have a Mass "For Persecuted Christians." Occasionally, we hear of religious persecution taking place in predominantly Muslim countries among the Christian minority and in communist countries, which place many restrictions on the free practice of religion. In some cases, various Christian groups are fighting each other over scarce resources and territorial issues. Consequently, there will be times when the news of persecution moves one to find an appropriate day to celebrate the Mass "For Persecuted Christians."

Third, we have a Mass "For a Spiritual or Pastoral Gathering." I often use this Mass when we have religious conventions in town and they want to begin their meetings with a Mass asking God's blessing upon their gathering. The second Collect of this Mass is very appropriate for such an occasion:

> O God, whose Son promised to all those gathered in
>   his name
> that he would be there in their midst,
> grant, we pray,
> that we may be aware of his presence among us
> and, in truth and charity, experience in our hearts
> an abundance of grace, mercy and peace.

Another occasion for the use of this Mass would be a day of renewal for a school board or parish council.

PART II: FOR CIVIL NEEDS

In this part of the Masses and Prayers for Various Needs and Occasions, you have a series of Masses based on possible civil needs, including prayers for elected officials, the beginning of the civil year, the sanctification of human labor, agricultural needs, the preservation of peace and justice, in time of war, and natural disasters. Once again, we have a section of the Missal that is seldom used. However, the needs addressed by the Masses in this section are very real.

How often do we pray for our public officials? Especially after an election, it would be good to ask God's blessings upon our public servants. Yet we sometimes get so tired of the long campaigns that lead up to elections that we forget to pray for those newly elected or re-elected. Nonetheless, the decisions these officials make and the personal example they set can have an immense impact on our lives and communities.

Since on New Year's Day we celebrate the Solemnity of Mary, the Holy Mother of God, we often forget to use the Mass

"At the Beginning of the Civil Year." Yet this Mass could be easily celebrated during one of the first weeks of a new year. Its prayers are not tied to January 1. This is clear in the Collect:

O God, who are without beginning or end,
the source of all creation,
grant us so to live this new year,
whose beginning we dedicate to you,
that we may abound in good things
and be resplendent with works of holiness.

It would be good to say a prayer at Mass at the beginning of a new year that reminds us to dedicate our efforts this coming year to doing good things and to living a holy life.

On Labor Day, we often use one of the two Masses "For the Sanctification of Human Labor." There are so many important themes that are connected with human labor: human progress, the spread of God's Kingdom, human dignity, creating unity in the human family, service of neighbor, sustaining our life on earth, practicing sincere charity, and sharing in the work of Christ. All these themes are referred to in one of the two Masses "For the Sanctification of Human Labor."

In rural areas, the Masses "At Seedtime" and "After the Harvest" can be important occasions to recognize the great service done for us by those working in agriculture. If you live in an area where people are working in the fields, recognizing the importance of their work and calling God's blessing upon them can be a welcome support to the intensity of their labor. Around Thanksgiving, we are reminded of God's bountiful goodness in the abundant crops and foods that we can purchase in our stores and shopping centers. Perhaps the Mass "After the Harvest" could be scheduled on an appropriate day prior to celebrating Thanksgiving.

The next group of Masses deals with issues of community and the quality of life we share in common. These Masses are "For the Progress of Peoples," "For the Preservation of Peace and Justice," "In Time of War or Civil Disturbance," and "For Refugees and Exiles." The Mass "For the Progress of Peoples" invites us to pray for the just advancement of our neighbor, for the removal of divisions, and for equity and justice. The Mass "For the Preservation of Peace and Justice" prays that "we may work without ceasing to establish that justice, which alone ensures true and lasting peace."

The Mass "In Time of War or Civil Disturbance" asks God to "banish violence swiftly from our midst / and to wipe away all tears, / so that we may all truly deserve to be called your children." The Mass "For Refugees and Exiles" asks God to "look with compassion on refugees and exiles, / on segregated persons and on lost children." It prays that God restore them to their homeland and "give us a kind heart for the needy and for strangers." Occasionally, communities serve as hosts to refugees and exiles from foreign countries, who have fled their homeland due to war, persecution, or injustice. The Mass "For Refugees and Exiles" would be perfect to support people who are needy and viewed as strangers in a foreign land.

The next group of Masses deals with natural disasters: "In Time of Famine or For Those Suffering Hunger," "In Time of Earthquake," "For Rain," "For Fine Weather," and "For an End to Storms." While many of these problems do not affect us personally, we all have heard reports of countries where famine has ravaged the population, cities and villages have been destroyed by earthquake, and devastation caused by too little or too much rain.

The scriptures sometimes talk about Jesus calling us to take care of the hungry and the thirsty. See, for example, Matthew 25:35: "I was hungry and you gave me food, I was thirsty and you gave me drink." Remember the earthquake that took place at the time of Jesus' death in Matthew 27:54: "The centurion and those with him who were keeping watch over Jesus saw the earthquake and what took place, [and] they were terrified and said: 'Truly this man was God's Son!'" Of course,

Jesus saved his disciples by calming a great storm on the Sea of Galilee when, according to Mark 4:37, "A great gale arose, and the waves beat into the boat, so that the boat was already being swamped."

If you look in a concordance of the Bible and check out the words "hungry," "thirsty," "earthquake," "storm," "rain," "drought," etc., you will find even more Scripture passages that could be enhanced by using one of the Masses for natural disasters. Sometimes, we forget to use resource books to help us locate Scripture passages whose themes are found in the prayers of this section of the Missal. Once we locate a particular passage, we can then check the index in the back of the *Lectionary for Mass* to find the days when these Scripture passages are used at daily Mass.

PART III: FOR VARIOUS OCCASIONS

This part of Masses and Prayers for Various Needs and Occasions is probably used more often than the previous section, "For Civil Needs." Many of the themes found in Part III appear with greater regularity in the readings from scripture (for example, forgiveness of sins, chastity, charity). These Masses also include groups that people frequently ask us to pray for: relatives and friends, the sick, and the dying. In addition, these Masses often address a particular intention that the congregation wishes us to pray for (for example, the grace of a happy death, a special need, or thanksgiving).

The Scriptures make reference to people caught in adultery, sexual sins, or acts which tarnish the dignity and rights of human beings. It would be good to use the Mass "For Chastity" when one of these Scripture readings is proclaimed. The prayers of this Mass are very well done. For example, the Prayer after Communion states:

> Through the Sacraments we have received, O Lord,
> may our heart and our body flourish anew

by a keen sense of modesty and renewed chastity,
so that what has passed our lips as food
we may possess in purity of heart.

Of course, the priest will need to address the virtue of
chastity in his homily. While this is not a popular subject and
may make some people uncomfortable, it is an important part of
the gospel call to live a holy life.

Earlier in this book, when I talked about the communal
Anointing of the Sick, I mentioned that we could make use of
either the Mass found in *Pastoral Care of the Sick* or the Mass
"For the Sick" in this section of *The Roman Missal*. The prayers
in the Mass "For the Sick" are very moving and speak directly
to the sufferings of the sick people gathered in church for the
anointing. For example, the second Collect of this Mass truly
puts into words the sentiments of the congregation:

Almighty ever-living God, eternal health of believers,
hear our prayers for your servants who are sick:
grant them, we implore you, your merciful help,
so that, with their health restored,
they may give you thanks in the midst of your Church.

This prayer is certain to strike a positive chord in the
hearts of those who hear it. It is too bad that we do not find
more occasions to use this Mass.

Sometimes, a person is diagnosed as having a terminal
disease. The family and the sick person know that death is coming, yet the sick person may be homebound for many months
before the day of death arrives. At times, people have asked me
to pray for an end to their suffering, that they might move on to
a life with God in heaven. What they are asking for is prayers
for the grace of a happy death.

The Mass "For the Grace of a Happy Death" could be a
great source of consolation to such a person and his or her family. It puts into words sentiments that we often find it difficult to
say. For example, the Collect is beautifully written:

O God, who have created us in your image
and willed that your Son should undergo
   death for our sake,
grant that those who call upon you
may be watchful in prayer at all times,
so that we may leave this world without stain of sin
and may merit to rest with joy in your merciful
   embrace.

This prayer contains strong images: Jesus' death, our calling for God's help, our commitment to pray at all times, our hope to leave the world without serious sin on our conscience, and resting with joy in God's merciful embrace. Moreover, there are messages and intentions expressed here that people need to speak as death approaches.

Finally, there is a wonderful set of two Masses that conclude Part III in "For Giving Thanks to God." If people are grateful that they have been saved from some tragedy (a sudden death due to a car accident) or natural disaster (the family not being home when the roof of the house collapsed), the Collect in Option A will speak to their situation:

O God, who always listen mercifully
to your servants in distress,
we humbly beseech you,
as we give thanks for your kindness,
that, free from all evil,
we may constantly serve you in gladness.

The Prayer over the Offerings speaks of "our deliverance from distress" and the Prayer after Communion speaks of being freed "from the bond of sin," restored in "strength" and advancing "without hindrance towards the hope of glory." "Therefore, this Mass will work best when there is some problem that has been overcome.

At times, priests are asked to celebrate a Mass of Thanksgiving for some accomplishment, blessing, goal achieved, or honor given to a particular person or group of people. The second Mass "For Giving Thanks to God" is suitable for such occasions. It recognizes that all that we have and really are should be viewed as God's gift to us. The Collect expresses this very powerfully:

> O God, the Father of every gift,
> we confess that all we have and are comes
>   down from you;
> teach us to recognize the effects of your
>   boundless care
> and to love you with a sincere heart and with
>   all our strength.

This prayer cautions us not to be unduly proud over our accomplishments or blessings, since we could do nothing if it were not for the gifts of God that we have received.

The Prayer after Communion petitions God that "being strengthened by gifts of courage and joy, we may serve you more devoutly and be worthy of still further blessings." Usually, people hope that their good fortune will continue, and the Prayer after Communion ends by expressing the hope that we will "be worthy of still further blessings." And so the Mass prayers provide a fitting Christian response to our desire to celebrate some accomplishment, blessing, goal achieved, or honor received. We give thanks to God, without whom nothing is possible.

In conclusion, the Masses and Prayers for Various Needs and Occasions contains some Masses that are only used occasionally, but are nonetheless of great importance to people in the community (for example, "For the Election of a Pope or a Bishop," "On the Fiftieth Anniversary of Marriage," "For the Sanctification of Human Labor," or "For the Grace of a Happy Death"). However, you will only make full use of the rich collection of Masse in this section of the Missal if you plan in advance, rather than relying on your memory to pick out one of these Masses when the occasion presents itself.

While the *Ordo* makes suggestions about when some of the Masses are suitable, its recommendations are not comprehensive enough to meet the needs of every community. Nothing can take the place of a liturgy committee looking over the Masses and Prayers for Various Needs and Occasions, picking out certain Masses that they want to be sure to celebrate this year (for example, "For a Council or a Synod," "At the Beginning of the Civil Year," "For Chastity," and "For the Sick"). Once you have found your list of Masses from this section of the Missal that you want to use, you need to find a day when there are no obligatory memorials, feasts, or solemnities. You also need to coordinate the themes of the prayers of the Mass selected with the scripture readings assigned to that day. If you do this advance planning, you will see the benefits of your efforts in the renewed interest and participation in the liturgy by the people who attend daily Mass.

QUESTIONS FOR CONTINUED REFLECTION

1. Is your liturgy committee involved in making recommendations about the use of Masses and Prayers for Various Needs and Occasions? Why or why not?

2. Have you prayed using one of the Masses and Prayers for Various Needs and Occasions? Which one of these Masses are you familiar with? Did you enjoy hearing these special prayers?

3. Would you like to use the Masses "For the Pope" or "For the Bishop" on the occasion of their anniversary of election or ordination? What benefits would come from celebrating such a Mass?

4. There are Masses for priests, for the anniversaries of priests, for religious, for the anniversaries of religious, and for ministers of the Church. Since vocations to the priesthood, the religious life, and lay ministry are important

to the future of the Church, would you like to use one of these Masses in order to encourage vocations and promote understanding of the roles of these ministers in the Church?

5. There are Masses for wedding anniversaries and for families. How familiar are members of your parish with these Masses? How often are they used?

6. What does your parish do to celebrate Christian unity? Are you aware of the Week of Prayer for Christian Unity each January? Is your parish involved with an ecumenical group of Christians that works together? Is your parish part of an ecumenical Thanksgiving service each year? What more can you or your parish do to promote Christian unity?

7. How often does your parish pray for public officials? When would you recommend such prayers? Why are these prayers necessary?

8. Does your parish make use of the Mass "At the Beginning of the Civil Year"? Would you like to see a regular day set aside at the beginning of each year to dedicate our efforts in the coming year to the service of God and living a holy life?

9. We have several Masses dealing with issues of community and quality of life ("For the Progress of Peoples," "For the Preservation of Peace and Justice," "In Time of War or Civil Disturbance," and "For Refugees and Exiles"). Are there concerns in your community that one of these Masses would address?

10. Has your parish made use of any of the Masses that deal with natural disasters such as famine, earthquake, rain, fire, and storms. If so, what was the occasion, and how did people respond to this topic being addressed at Mass?

11. Would you like to see the Mass "For Chastity" used at your parish? Why or why not?

12. Has your parish made use of the Mass "For the Sick"? What was the occasion? A communal Anointing of the Sick? A day on which you commissioned new ministers of care to bring Communion to the sick? An epidemic that struck your town, causing many people to be sick in bed?

13. There is a beautiful Mass "For the Grace of a Happy Death." What type of catechesis needs to be done (for example, a pamphlet on ministering to those near to death or a homily on ministry to the dying) in order for people to feel comfortable celebrating such a Mass?

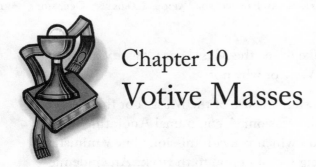

Chapter 10
Votive Masses

The word *votive* is the adjective form of the Latin word *votum*, which means a prayer, vow, or desire. In a liturgical context, it refers to a Mass celebrated at the wish or desire of the priest on days when there is no particular Mass assigned. The texts for these Masses honor God: for example, "The Most Holy Trinity" or "The Mercy of God," the angels, a saint (such as Mary, Joseph, or John the Baptist), or even all the saints.

The *General Instruction of the Roman Missal*, 375 explains Votive Masses in this way:

> Votive Masses of the mysteries of the Lord or in honor of the Blessed Virgin Mary or of the Angels or of any given Saint or of all the Saints may be said in response to the devotion of the faithful on weekdays in Ordinary Time, even if an Optional Memorial occurs. However, it is not permitted to celebrate as Votive Masses those that refer to mysteries related to events in the life of the Lord or of the Blessed Virgin Mary, with the exception of the Mass of the Immaculate Conception, since their celebration is an integral part of the course of the liturgical year.

There are nineteen Votive Masses contained in *The Roman Missal*. The main factor in selecting one of these Masses is the pastoral or devotional need of the faith community with whom the Mass will be celebrated.[1]

---

1. The introduction to Votive Masses in *The Roman Missal* offers this guidance: "If some serious pastoral benefit is to be gained, an appropriately corresponding Votive Mass may be used, at the discretion of the Ordinary, or with his permission, except on

With the freedom to choose one of these Masses on days when there is no particular Mass assigned (i.e., no obligatory memorial, feast, or solemnity), there are many occasions when the use of a Votive Mass is appropriate. Consequently, a schedule should be created to ensure that the spiritual and devotional needs of the local community are served by occasionally using one of the Masses in this section of *The Roman Missal*. The liturgy committee could assist the priest in putting together such a calendar of votive Masses.

The twenty-two Votive Masses in *The Roman Missal* are as follows:

1. The Most Holy Trinity
2. The Mercy of God
3. Our Lord Jesus Christ, the Eternal High Priest
4. The Mystery of the Holy Cross
5. The Most Holy Eucharist
6. The Most Holy Name of Jesus
7. The Most Precious Blood of Our Lord Jesus Christ
8. The Most Sacred Heart of Jesus
9. The Holy Spirit
10. The Blessed Virgin Mary
    Our Lady, Mother of the Church
    The Most Holy Name of Mary
    Our Lady, Queen of Apostles
11. The Holy Angels
12. Saint John the Baptist
13. Saint Joseph
14. All the Holy Apostles
15. Saints Peter and Paul, Apostles
16. Saint Peter, Apostle
17. Saint Paul, Apostle
18. One Holy Apostle
19. All Saints

Solemnities, on the Sundays of Advent, Lent, and Easter, on the days within the Octave of Easter, on the Commemoration of All the Faithful Departed (All Souls' Day), on Ash Wednesday, and on the weekdays of Holy Week."

While we celebrate the Solemnity of the Most Holy Trinity each year on the Sunday after Pentecost, the mystery of the Holy Trinity is such an important doctrine that this Votive Mass can be celebrated on some other fitting occasion during the year. The Collect for this Mass contains not only good theology but a language that lends itself to a sense of mystery and awe, which is one of the hallmarks of the Roman tradition of prayer:

> God our Father, who, by sending into the world
> the Word of truth and the Spirit of sanctification,
> made known to the human race your wondrous mystery
> grant us, we pray, that in professing the true faith
> we may acknowledge the Trinity of eternal glory
> and adore your Unity, powerful in majesty.

People will benefit from hearing this beautiful prayer. Its eloquence can touch their minds and hearts in giving glory and praise to God.

The special Preface provided with the Votive Mass for "The Most Holy Trinity" provides a wonderful explanation of the mystery of this doctrine:

> For with your Only Begotten Son and the Holy Spirit
> you are one God, one Lord:
> not in the unity of a single person,
> but in a Trinity of one substance.

> For what you have revealed to us of your glory
> we believe equally of your Son
> and of the Holy Spirit,
> so that, in the confessing of the true and
>   eternal Godhead
> you might be adored in what is proper to each Person,
> their unity in substance,
> and their equality in majesty.

This Preface provides a beautiful outline for a homily on the Trinity as well as a prayer of praise in honor of the mystery of the Trinity.

The mercy of God is another theme that appears often in the readings assigned to daily Mass. If you use a biblical concordance and look up the words "mercy" or "forgiveness," you will be led to a long list of occurrences where these themes are found in scripture. Then all you will need to do is refer to the index of readings found in the *Lectionary for Mass* and find the days during the liturgical year in which these readings are proclaimed at Mass. The theme of God's mercy is also found in the Votive Masses. The Collect for the Votive Mass for "The Mercy of God" is poetic and inspiring and emphasizes the infinite love of God:

> O God, whose mercies are without number
> and whose treasure of goodness is infinite,
> graciously increase the faith of the people consecrated
>   to you,
> that all may grasp and rightly understand
> by whose love they have been created,
> through whose Blood they have been redeemed,
> and by whose Spirit they have been reborn.

The next six Votive Masses all deal with sacred mysteries from the life of our Lord Jesus Christ:

- Our Lord Jesus Christ, the Eternal High Priest
- The Mystery of the Holy Cross
- The Most Holy Eucharist
- The Most Holy Name of Jesus
- The Most Precious Blood of Our Lord Jesus Christ
- The Most Sacred Heart of Jesus

In each case, there are scripture readings for daily Mass that contain these themes. We simply have to spend a little time looking up passages with these themes, either by referencing the index in the *Lectionary for Mass* or by using a biblical concordance.

The prayers of the Mass on "The Mystery of the Holy Cross" provide numerous references that unpack this great mystery: saving the human race; the instrument of redemption; a sacred oblation offered on the altar of the Cross, cancelling the offenses of the whole world and cleansing us of all our sins; the life-giving tree, the tree that conquered the evil one; and the life-giving Cross. There is also a special Preface for this Mass, whose poetry and biblical imagery are quite moving:

> For you placed the salvation of the human race
> in the wood of the Cross,
> so that, where death arose,
> life might again spring forth
> and the evil one, who conquered on a tree,
> might likewise on a tree be conquered,
> through Christ our Lord.

I think of all the times I read the Gospels in which Jesus predicted his Death and Resurrection and regret that I did not make use of this beautiful Mass. Yet if I had spent just a little time looking up "Death" and "Cross" in my biblical concordance, I would have made use of the Mass on "The Mystery of the Holy Cross" to the pastoral advantage of the members of my community.

It is not difficult to find opportunities for using the Mass on "The Most Holy Eucharist." All the Gospel accounts have stories about the miraculous feeding of large groups of people; these stories anticipate the spiritual feeding of the soul that takes place with each celebration of the Eucharist. Then there are the Gospel accounts in John with the famous "Bread of Life" discourse. Consequently, there are numerous places where this wonderful Mass of the Most Holy Eucharist could be used to the spiritual advantage of the faithful.

While all the prayers of the Mass for the Most Holy Eucharist are rich in theology, poetry, and biblical references, I was especially moved by the Prayer over the Offerings:

> Celebrating the memorial of our salvation,
> we humbly beseech your mercy, O Lord,
> that this Sacrament of your loving kindness
> may be for us the sign of unity and the bond of charity.

"Mercy," "loving kindness," "unity," "charity"—these are themes that speak to the needs of people today as well as themes that will facilitate the prayer of the worshipping community.

Through the centuries, numerous devotions to the various names and titles given to Jesus have developed because of the strong faith of true believers. Think of all the titles given to Jesus: Man of Suffering (Isaiah 53:3); Emmanuel (Matthew 1:23); the Nazarene (Matthew 2:23); Son of Mary (Mark 6:3); Word of God (John 1:1); True Light (John 1:9); God the only Son of the Father (John 1:18, 3:16); Lamb of God (John 1:29); Son of Joseph (John 1:45); Son of God, King of Israel (John 1:49); Savior of the World (John 4:42); Bread of Life (John 6:35); Light of the World (John 8:12); Good Shepherd (John 10:11); the Resurrection and the Life (John 11:25); the Way, the Truth, and the Life (John 14:6); the Holy and Just One (Acts 3:14); and many others. Yet one name stands out among all the titles and names given to our Lord: the most holy name of Jesus.

Philippians 2:10–11 tells us: "At the name of Jesus every knee should bend in heaven, on earth, and under the earth, and every tongue confess that Jesus Christ is Lord, to the glory of God the Father." The name "Jesus" is the Greek version of the Hebrew name "Yeshua," or Joshua. "Jesus" or "Joshua" means "Yahweh is salvation." This meaning is alluded to in Matthew 1:21 ("She is to have a son, and you are to name him Jesus, because he will save his people from their sins.") and in Luke 2:21 ("After eight days had passed, it was time to circumcise the child, and he was called Jesus, the name given by the angel before he was conceived in the womb.").[2] Knowing the etymology of the name of Jesus is helpful when coming to appreciate the reverence that people have for Our Lord's holy name.

Since people are often identified with their names, people saw pronouncing the name of Jesus as a way to talk about the character, authority, and sacred nature of Our Lord, the only

---

2. The title "Christ" means "the anointed one." Sometimes, people confuse the meaning of "Jesus" with the meaning of "Christ."

begotten Son of God. Of course, the Apostles performed miracles and exorcisms "in the name of Jesus," that is, by his authority and power (see Mark 9:38; Acts 4:30). Moreover, Acts 2:38 quotes Saint Peter as saying: "Repent and be baptized, every one of you, in the name of Jesus Christ, so that your sins may be forgiven; and you will receive the gift of the Holy Spirit." In 1 Corinthians 6:11, Saint Paul reminds us of the power at work in Jesus' name: "But you were washed, you were sanctified, you were justified in the name of our Lord Jesus Christ and in the Spirit of our God." No wonder the first Christians felt so strongly that the name of Jesus be given the respect and veneration that it so richly deserves.

As there developed a great love for the name of Jesus, so too there developed a great devotion to the Most Precious Blood of our Lord Jesus Christ. Of course, by shedding his Blood Jesus won for us the gift of salvation. This theology is captured in the Collect:

> O God, who by the Precious Blood of your
>   Only Begotten Son
> have redeemed the whole world,
> preserve in us the work of your mercy,
> so that, ever honoring the mystery of salvation,
> we may merit to obtain its fruits.

This Collect builds on the text from the Book of Revelation 5:9–10, which is also the antiphon of this Mass: "You have redeemed us, Lord, by your Blood, / from every tribe and tongue and people and nation, / and made us into a kingdom for our God."

In the Old Testament, blood was identified with the life of a living being (see Genesis 9:4; Deuteronomy 12:23). At the same time, the Jews also believed that life was a gift of God and under his dominion or rule. In sacrificial ritual, blood represented the life God had given to us, and it was symbolically offered to God by pouring it on the altar (representing God) or sprinkling it before the sanctuary (Leviticus 1:5; 4:6). Of course, the blood of the Passover lamb was smeared on the doorposts of the house where the Passover supper was celebrated (Exodus 12:7, 13), thus protecting the inhabitants from the angel of death. Blood was also sprinkled on the people, signifying that God's covenanted people shared a common life with God (Exodus 24:6).

What was unique about the Blood of the Eucharist was that Jesus told us to drink his Blood rather than sprinkle it on the assembly as the Jews would do. Obviously, Jesus wanted us to know that we share his very life when we eat his Body and drink his Blood (John 6:53; 1 Corinthians 10:16). Moreover, Jesus calls his Blood the "blood of the new and eternal covenant"—an allusion to Exodus 24:8 ("Then Moses took the blood and dashed it on the people, saying, "See the blood of the covenant which the Lord has made with you in accordance with all these words.") And so, references to the Most Precious Blood of Christ also flow into reminders that we are part of a new Covenant that has been sealed by the Blood of the Lamb, who was sacrificed for our redemption. Hence, the Votive Mass for "The Most Precious Blood of Our Lord Jesus Christ" has a rich biblical basis.

The final Mass in this section on the mysteries of Our Lord's life is for "The Most Sacred Heart of Jesus." This Mass is usually said on the Friday following the celebration of the Solemnity of the Most Holy Body and Blood of Christ (*Corpus Christi*). The theme of this Mass is focused upon the love of Jesus, symbolized in his wounded heart. Devotion to the Sacred Heart of Jesus first appears in the writings of Saint Gertrude (1256–1302), a sister of the Benedictine monastery in Helfta, Germany. Saint Gertrude received the stigmata and a revelation from the Lord regarding the heart of Christ, which was pierced by the soldier's lance. She often meditated on the sufferings and passion of Christ and the pain he endured for our salvation.

Saint Margaret Mary Alacocque (1648–1690) gave new impetus to the devotion to the Sacred Heart when she experienced a series of visions of the Sacred Heart of Jesus. In the last of these visions that Jesus revealed to Saint Margaret Mary, he expressed the desire to establish a feast of the Sacred Heart on the Friday after the octave of *Corpus Christi*. Many argue that this devotion traces to the early theology of the Church, which emphasized that the wounded side of Jesus was the source of all graces. The blood that poured out from his side came from his heart, overflowing with love for God's people. I encourage Priest Celebrants and liturgy committees to investigate more of the history behind this powerful devotion to the Sacred Heart as part of their preparation to celebrate this wonderful feast day.

The next group of Masses in this section of the Missal celebrates the working of the Holy Spirit in the minds and hearts of faithful people. There are three Masses presented in honor of the Holy Spirit. The first two options have their own special Preface. The prayers in these Masses for the Holy Spirit can be very helpful in gaining a deeper appreciation of the role of the Holy Spirit in in the life of the Church. Given the large number of references to the working of the Holy Spirit, there should be no shortage of opportunities to make use of these Masses. Again, refer to the index of readings in the *Lectionary for Mass* to find when the theme of the Holy Spirit is evident in the readings. If there is no obligatory Mass, the Masses for the Holy Spirit will be most appropriate on these days.

One place to find scripture readings that would go well with one of the Masses of the "The Holy Spirit" is in the antiphons assigned to each Mass. All the Entrance and Communion Antiphons are quotes from scripture: Romans 5:5; Romans 8:11; Psalm 67:29–30; John 14:26; John 15:26; John 16:14; Luke 4:18; Psalm 103:30. If you consult the index to the *Lectionary for Mass* to learn when a reading contains one of these scripture references, you will generate a list of possible days when using a Mass of the Holy Spirit makes good sense. Finally, many schools celebrate at the beginning of a new school year a Mass of the Holy Spirit. I believe you will find these three Masses will work well your students, since they often speak of the "light of the Holy Spirit," helping us to become "truly wise," "enlightening our minds," "lead[ing] us into all truth," and moving us "to love," to possess a "right spirit," and a "heart" to God's will.

The next group of Masses in this section of the Missal is dedicated to Mary. Option A refers you to the Commons, where there are 11 Masses for Mary. Option B is a Mass that celebrates an important theme: "Our Lady, Mother of the Church." Option C is the popular Mass "The Most Holy Name of Mary." Option D celebrates "Our Lady, Queen of Apostles." Let's look at the three new Masses in this section.

Referring to Mary as "Our Lady, Mother of the Church" goes back to the words of Jesus on the Cross to Mary and Saint John (John 19: 26-27): "Woman, here is your son. . . . Here is your mother." On March 25, 1987, Pope John Paul II published a beautiful encyclical on Mary, entitled *Redemptoris Mater (The Mother of the Redeemer): On the Blessed Virgin Mary in the Life of the Pilgrim Church*. I highly encourage you to read again this powerful statement of the role of Mary in human history and the life of the Church. In *Redemptoris Mater*, 24, Pope John Paul II explains the title "Our Lady, Mother of the Church:"

> The words uttered by Jesus from the Cross signify
> that the motherhood of her who bore Christ finds
> a "new" continuation in the Church and through
> the Church, symbolized and represented by John.
> In this way, she who is the one "full of grace" was
> brought into the mystery of Christ in order to be his
> Mother and thus the Holy Mother of God, through
> the Church remains in that mystery as "the woman"
> spoken of by the Book of Genesis (3:15) at the begin-
> ning and by the Apocalypse (12:1) at the end of the
> history of salvation. In accordance with the eternal
> plan of Providence, Mary's divine motherhood is
> to be poured out upon the Church, as indicated by
> statements of Tradition, according to which Mary's

"motherhood" of the Church is the reflection and
extension of her motherhood of the Son of God. . . .

Thus she who is present in the mystery of Christ as
Mother becomes—by the will of the Son and the
power of the Holy Spirit—present in the mystery of
the Church. In the Church too she continues to be a
maternal presence, as is shown by the words spoken
from the Cross: "Woman, behold your son! . . . Behold,
your mother."

The above paragraphs are just a sample of a more extensive
explanation that Pope John Paul II provides on the special role
of Mary as Mother of the Church.

Of course, this Mass can be used on Saturday or on
occasions when the scriptures speak of Mary's divine maternity.
Option B contains a special Preface that expands on this theme
in a powerful way:

Receiving your Word in her Immaculate Heart,
she was found worthy to conceive him in
    her virgin's womb
and, giving birth to the Creator,
she nurtured the beginnings of the Church.

Standing beside the Cross,
she received the testament of divine love
and took to herself as sons and daughters
all those who by the Death of Christ
are born to heavenly life.

As the Apostles awaited the Spirit you had promised,
she joined her supplication to the prayers of the disciples
and so became the pattern of the Church at prayer.

Raised to the glory of heaven,
she accompanies your pilgrim Church
    with a mother's love

and watches in kindness over the Church's
   homeward steps,
until the Lord's Day shall come in glorious splendor.

What a magnificent explanation of the important role that Mary
plays in the life of the Church! This Mass will truly benefit the
spiritual lives of all who hear these beautiful prayers.

   Option C contains the Mass of "The Most Holy Name
of Mary." As with the Most Holy Name of Jesus, so too the
Church began to venerate the name of Mary because of the criti-
cal role she played in God's plan of salvation and her courageous
living as a woman of great faith. The Collect makes this very
clear when it says:

O God, who chose the Blessed Virgin Mary,
full of grace, from among women
to become the Mother of your Son, our Redeemer,
mercifully grant that, venerating her holy name,
we may escape the dangers of this present age
and obtain with her life eternal.

This Collect and the other prayers of this Mass are based on
sound biblical theology and express our Catholic beliefs in a
poetic and pleasing manner that appeals to the minds and hearts
of God's people. I recommend that you consider using this Mass
on days when the following scripture readings are used: Judith
13:18–19 (from the Entrance Antiphon) and Luke 1:26–27
(from the Communion Antiphon).

   Option D contains the Mass for "Our Lady, Queen of
Apostles." Of course, on August 22 we celebrate the Memorial
of the Queenship of the Blessed Virgin Mary. This Mass adds to
the title of "Queen" the reference to the Apostles. The Collect
reminds us that Mary was with the Apostles on Pentecost, praying with them for the coming of the Holy Spirit. She supported
the Apostles by word and example in their work of proclaiming
the Gospel to the ends of the world. In the Prayer over the
Offerings, we pray for the grace that the Church "may grow in

the number of the faithful / and be ever radiant with an abundance of virtues." This Mass could be used when these scripture readings are read: Acts 1:14 (from the Entrance Antiphon) and Luke 11:27–28 (from the Communion Antiphon). Traditionally, the celebration of "Our Lady, Queen of Apostles" has taken place on the Saturday after the Solemnity of the Ascension of the Lord.

The title "Queen of Apostles" became popular in the twentieth century. On November 1, 1954, Pope Pius XII established a yearly celebration of the Queenship of Mary on May 31. After Vatican II, this Mass was moved to August 22. The title "Queen" comes from our belief that Mary is Queen of heaven and earth, due to her divine calling to be the Mother of the Savior. Since the powerful image of Mary in the midst of the Apostles at Pentecost occurs each year, the tradition of referring to Mary as Queen of Apostles became popular and eventually resulted in the creation of the Mass of "Our Lady, Queen of Apostles."

There is only one Mass for the Holy Angels. Of course, there are specified days when we celebrate the role of the angels in salvation history: Saints Michael, Gabriel, and Raphael, Archangels, on September 29; and the Holy Guardian Angels on October 2. In many of our Marian Masses, we use the Gospel from Luke 1:26, where the angel Gabriel announces to Mary that she is to the mother of the Savior. Yet, there are many other places in scripture where angels figure prominently, especially in these Gospel accounts: Matthew 1:20; Matthew 2:13, 19; Matthew 2:24, 28; Matthew 4:11; Matthew 13:39; Matthew 18:10; Matthew 25:31; Mark 8:38; Luke 1:1; Luke 2:9; Luke 2:15; Luke 16:22; Luke 24:23; John 20:12. If you look up these passages in the index of your Lectionary, you will find a large number of days when reference is made to angels.

The last group of Masses in this section of *The Roman Missal* celebrates the lives of saints: Saint John the Baptist, Saint Joseph, All the Holy Apostles, Saints Peter and Paul, Saint Peter,

Saint Paul, One Holy Apostle, and All Saints. While all these Masses also have special celebrations on particular days of the liturgical year, the importance of these saints in the life of the Church deserves additional recognition by the use of these Masses on days when the scripture readings are appropriate.

The easiest way to find a day when the scripture readings would complement the use of one of these Masses in honor of the saints is to look at the scripture citations in *The Roman Missal* for the Entrance Antiphon and the Communion Antiphon. Find the scripture passages in the index of the *Lectionary* that correspond to these passages. If you need additional days when the celebration of one of these saints would be appropriate, you can also look up their name in a biblical concordance.

The Masses in this section of the Missal offer much food for thought and inspiration. In fact, the Masses for Saint John the Baptist, Saint Joseph, and Saints Peter and Paul have special Prefaces that you can use when their Mass is celebrated. As another alternative to using the Mass for Saint Joseph in this section of the Missal, the rubrics note the following: "If appropriate, the Mass of the Solemnity, as on March 19, or of Saint Joseph the Worker, as on May 1, may also be said." When using the Mass for "One Holy Apostle," the rubrics note: "In this Mass, the color red is used. The Mass of his feast is said. But if he is honored together with another Apostle and the texts of the Mass are not appropriate for that Apostle, the following Mass is said with the color red." If you believe that more could be said about a particular Apostle than is found in some of the joint Masses of significant saints (e.g., Saints Peter and Paul), then the Mass for "One Holy Apostle" may be used on another occasion, when the scripture readings are appropriate to that particular Apostle.

Finally, there is another Mass, for "All Saints," in this section of the Missal, that provides an additional option to the Mass assigned to November 1 on the Solemnity of All Saints.

At times, the scripture readings speak of our calling to live as saints. It would be spiritually advantageous for the prayer life of our people to hear the Collect from this Mass:

> O God, fount of all holiness,
> make us each walk worthily in our vocation,
> through the intercession of your Saints,
> on whom you bestowed
> a great variety of graces on earth
> and a single glorious reward in heaven.

This prayer asks God to make us worthy servants on earth as he did with his saints in heaven. In this way, it expresses a prayer that is often in the hearts of our people.

Where would you find a scripture passage during the week that would work well with the Mass for "All Saints"? There is a popular passage from Colossians 3:12 that says: "As God's chosen ones, holy and beloved, clothe yourselves with compassion, kindness, humility, meekness, and patience." If you are looking for scripture passages that speak about our calling to live as saints, then check your biblical concordance for these words: "saints," "chosen ones," "holy people," and "a people set apart." The Communion Antiphon from this Mass is based on the Beatitudes, Matthew 5:8–10, which come up more than once each liturgical year. Hence, there are many occasions when the beautiful and inspiring prayers of this Mass may be used.

In summary, the section on Votive Masses in *The Roman Missal* has a treasury of beautiful, inspiring Masses that people who attend daily Mass would find beneficial in strengthening their life of faith. Votive Masses celebrate themes connected directly to God (the Most Holy Trinity and the Mercy of God), the mysteries of Our Lord Jesus Christ (Our Lord Jesus Christ, the Eternal High Priest; the Mystery of the Holy Cross; the Most Holy Eucharist, etc.), the working of the Holy Spirit; the importance of Mary (Our Lady, Mother of the Church; the Most Holy Name of Mary; Our Lady, Queen of Apostles), the work of the Holy Angels; the work of special saints; and all the saints. I encourage priests and liturgy committees to find days during the week when these Masses may be used to the benefit of the faithful.

QUESTIONS FOR CONTINUED REFLECTION

1. What is the main factor that a priest or liturgy committee should consider in choosing to celebrate a Votive Mass?

2. Do you consider the Mystery of the Trinity and the Mercy of God important truths of the faith, truths warranting additional attention during the week when the scripture readings are suitable?

3. Which of the six Masses celebrating mysteries in the life of Jesus would you most want to see celebrated during the week? Why?

4. Does your parish foster devotion to the Sacred Heart of Jesus? Do you have a shrine to the Sacred Heart of Jesus in your church?

5. The working of the Holy Spirit is a mystery that most communities need to consider on a regular basis. When would be a good occasion to make use of one of the Masses of the Holy Spirit?

6. Have you ever celebrated in your parish one of the Votive Masses for Mary? Would you like to do this? If so, why?

7. Which of the special Masses for saints do you think you and your fellow parishioners would like to celebrate in your parish? Why?

Chapter 11
Masses for the Dead

The last section of *The Roman Missal* contains the Masses for the Dead. This includes funeral Masses, Masses on the anniversary of a death, various commemorations ("For One Deceased Person," "For Several Deceased Persons or for All the Dead"), and Various Prayers for the Dead (for example, "For a Pope," a "For a Bishop," "For a Young Person," etc.) The intention in designing this section of the Missal was to provide Masses that would cover the full range of circumstances under which a funeral or a memorial Mass takes place.

   One of the reforms of Vatican II that has been most successful is the *Order of Christian Funerals*, which has three main parts: the Vigil for the Deceased or wake service, the funeral Mass or Liturgy outside Mass, and the Rite of Committal or the interment service. While the prayers in the *Order of Christian Funerals* have not been revised, the prayers for funerals and memorial Masses have been revised in this section of *The Roman Missal*. Consequently, it would be best for the Priest Celebrant to use the Masses for funerals and memorials that are found in *The Roman Missal*. Of course, the priest is free to continue using the other services and prayers in the *Order of Christian Funerals* until a new revision has been issued.

   In the General Introduction to the *Order of Christian Funerals*, 4–6, we are reminded of the reasons for celebrating a Catholic funeral liturgy:

> At the death of a Christian, whose life of faith was
> begun in the waters of baptism and strengthened at the
> eucharistic table, the Church intercedes on behalf of

the deceased because of its confident belief that death is not the end, nor does it break the bonds forged in life. The Church also ministers to the sorrowing and consoles them in the funeral rites with the comforting word of God and the sacrament of the Eucharist.

Christians celebrate the funeral rites to offer worship, praise, and thanksgiving to God for the gift of a life which has now been returned to God, the author of life and the hope of the just. The Mass, the memorial of Christ's death and resurrection, is the principal celebration of the Christian funeral.

The Church through its funeral rites commends the dead to God's merciful love and pleads for the forgiveness of their sins. At the funeral rites, especially at the celebration of the Eucharistic sacrifice, the Christian community affirms and expresses the union of the Church on earth with the Church in heaven in the one great communion of saints. Though separated from the living, the dead are still at one with the community of believers on earth and benefit from their prayers and intercession. At the rite of final commendation and farewell, the community acknowledges the reality of separation and commends the deceased to God. In this way it recognizes the spiritual bond that still exists between the living and the dead and proclaims its belief that all the faithful will be raised up and reunited in the new heavens and a new earth, where death will be no more.

I have always found the General Introduction to the *Order of Christian Funerals* to be an immensely helpful document that warrants our reading over and over in order to be certain that we are truly fulfilling the Church's desire to bring hope and consolation to the grieving family and friends.

Since there may be some confusion about what prayers to use when celebrating a funeral or memorial Mass, let me clarify that the prayers for Mass should come from *The Roman Missal*. The Masses covered in this section of *The Roman Missal* are the following:

     I. For the Funeral
        Outside Easter Time (2 Masses, 4 Collects)
        During Easter Time (1 Mass, 2 Collects)
        Other Prayers for the Funeral Mass (1 Mass,
            1 Collect)
        For the Funeral of a Baptized Child (2 Masses)
        For the Funeral of a Child Who Died Before
            Baptism (1 Mass, 2 Collects)
    II. On the Anniversary
        Outside Easter Time (1 Mass)
        During Easter Time (1 Mass)
        Other Prayers on the Anniversary (2 Masses)
   III. Various Commemorations
        For One Deceased Person (5 Masses, 6 Collects)
        For Several Deceased Persons or For All the Dead
            (9 Masses)
   IV. Various Prayers for the Dead
        For a Pope (3 Masses)
        For a Bishop (2 Masses)
        For a Priest (2 Masses)
        For a Deacon (1 Mass)
        For a Religious (1 Mass)
        For One Who Worked in the Service of the Gospel
            (1 Collect)
        For a Young Person (1 Collect)
        For One Who Suffered a Long Illness (1 Collect)
        For One Who Died Suddenly (1 Collect)
        For a Married Couple (1 Collect if both spouses
            are deceased and 1 Collect if only one spouse is
            deceased and the other still living)
        For the Priest's Parents (1 Mass)
        For Relatives, Friends, and Benefactors (1 Mass)

All priests, deacons, and members of liturgy or bereavement committees that are involved in preparing the funeral or memorial Mass should be familiar with the Masses in this section of *The Roman Missal*. In the list above, you sometimes find more Collects listed than Masses. This is because some Masses have two options for the Collect. Some options in "Various Prayers for the Dead" only provide a Collect. In those cases, the Prayer over the Offerings and the Prayer after Communion are found in one of the Masses in Parts I, II, or III.

Given the great number of prayers to choose from, a priest can sometimes forget that the Church has provided a special Collect for a young person, for one who has died suddenly, or a deceased spouse when the other spouse is still living and present at the liturgy. The assistance of a member of the bereavement committee, the liturgy committee, a liturgy coordinator, a deacon, or a pastoral associate can be most helpful in providing the priest with guidance in choosing the best possible prayer for the particular circumstance. I have founded several bereavement committees in different parishes that I have served in, and I always found the people who are called to this ministry to be a great assistance in caring for the grieving and in preparing the funeral liturgy.

There is even a Mass for a priest's parents, if they are both deceased. If the priest's parents died together suddenly in an accident, then this Mass can be celebrated as is on the day of their funeral or on their joint anniversary of death. The priest can also choose to celebrate this Mass on one of the anniversary days of death of either his father or mother. In addition, on an anniversary day of a parent's death, the priest can choose to use one of the anniversary Masses listed in Part II.

In surveys that have been done on services provided at the time of death, our Catholic *Order of Christian Funerals* has always fared well. In part, this is due to the hopeful, comforting, joyful tone of so many of the prayers used during the three major liturgies: at the wake, at the church, and at the cemetery. It is also due to the tremendous investment of self on the part of priests, deacons, musicians, and bereavement and liturgy committee members. It is interesting that when television news runs a story about death, they almost invariably show a clip taken from a Catholic funeral Mass. Let me share with you a few of the beautiful prayers that are found in the Masses for the Dead.

In Part I, "For a Funeral Mass Outside Easter Time," the second Collect in Option A often strikes a positive chord in the people who hear it:

> O God, whose nature
> is always to forgive and to show mercy,
> we humbly implore you for your servant N.,
> whom you have called (this day) to journey to you,
> and, since he (she) hoped and believed in you,
> grant that he (she) may be led to our true homeland
> to delight in its everlasting joys.

At the time of death, people sometimes worry about the sins committed by the deceased. Hence, the reference to God's forgiveness and mercy speaks to the cares of many people. The metaphors "journey to you" and "true homeland" speak to people's understanding of the meaning of life. The words "hoped," "believed" and "everlasting joys" speak to the faith that a baptized person has in the promises of the risen Christ.

In the Mass "For the Funeral of a Baptized Child," the Collect addresses the terrible pain and sorrow of the grieving family by reminding us that God's wisdom is beyond earthly wisdom. Although we have lost a young child, we know that he or she has been adopted by God in Baptism. We look forward to the day when we will be reunited in God's Kingdom. The Collect of the first Mass in this category says:

> Most compassionate God,
> who in the counsels of your wisdom
> have called this little child to yourself
> on the very threshold of life,
> listen kindly to our prayers

and grant that one day we may inherit eternal life
    with him (her),
whom, by the grace of Baptism, you have adopted as
    your own child
and who we believe is dwelling even now in your
    Kingdom.

There is no easy answer to the questions: Why did this young child die? Why didn't God do something to save him or her? However, by placing these questions in the context of faith and divine providence, the Collect provides the beginning of an approach that can help us move beyond these questions to embrace the wisdom of God.

When you need to use the Mass "For the Funeral of a Child Who Died Before Baptism," you may encounter feelings of worry and even guilt that the parents did not have the chance to baptize the baby. In these cases, I ask the parents if they intended to baptize the baby. Usually, they say "yes" and explain that the child was sick at birth but was expected to recover. I affirm that there is a Baptism of desire by the part of the parents and the Church that God will surely take into account. The rubrics for this Mass note that "in funerals of this kind there should ordinarily be a Liturgy of the Word, as described in the Roman ritual. Nevertheless, if at times the celebration of Mass is judged opportune, the following texts should be used." The second Collect of this Mass is pastorally sensitive:

O God, searcher of hearts and most loving consoler,
who know the faith of these parents,
grant that, as they mourn their child,
now departed from this life,
they may be assured
that he (she) has been entrusted to
    your divine compassion.

The Prayer after Communion asks God "to comfort amid the sorrows of this life / those whom you have graciously nourished / by these sacred mysteries, / so as to strengthen their hope of life eternal." These prayers speak eloquently to the needs, hopes, and tears of the grieving parents.

In Part II, there are four Masses on the anniversary of the death of a loved one. The rubric in *The Roman Missal* gives a special permission for the first anniversary of death: "This Mass may be celebrated on the *first* anniversary even on days within the Octave of the Nativity of the Lord, and on days when an Obligatory Memorial occurs and on weekdays, with the exception of Ash Wednesday and weekdays during Holy Week" (emphasis added). For other anniversaries, the rubric states: "On other anniversaries, this Mass may be celebrated on weekdays in Ordinary Time even when an Optional Memorial occurs." And so, there is a great deal of freedom granted for the celebration of Masses on the anniversary of death.

The Collect for the anniversary Mass Outside Easter Time is short, direct, and draws on biblical imagery (the dew of God's mercy). This prayer says:

> Send down, we pray, O Lord
> the lasting dew of your mercy on your servant N.,
> whose anniversary we commemorate,
> and be pleased to grant him (her)
> the company of your Saints.

I like the metaphor of dew. It reminds me of early mornings, when a heavy dew is on the grass. If you walk through the grass, your shoes get thoroughly soaked. This prayer asks God to send down the dew of his mercy, that it might thoroughly transform (soak into) our loved ones and make them part of the company of saints. The beauty of this imagery can speak to the hearts of God's people.

Part III on Various Commemorations contains five Masses "For One Deceased Person" and nine Masses "For Several Deceased Persons or For All the Dead." The rubrics at the beginning of Part III note the following:

This Mass may be celebrated when the news of a death is first received or on the day of final burial, even on days within the Octave of the Nativity of the Lord, on days when an Obligatory Memorial occurs, and on weekdays, with the exception of Ash Wednesday and weekdays during Holy Week.

"Daily" Masses for the Dead may be celebrated on weekdays in Ordinary Time, even if an Optional Memorial occurs, provided such Masses are actually applied for the dead.

Consequently, there is broad leeway granted for the use of these various commemorations. I believe the rubrics give us a hint of the type of occasion when these Masses could be used: "when the news of a death is first received." Sometimes, we hear of the death of a person whose funeral Mass is being celebrated at another parish. Sometimes, the news of the person's death reaches us after the funeral. Many people in the parish feel a sense of loss, since this person spent many years working in your parish—for example, as a director of religious education or a pastoral associate. It would be appropriate and pastorally sensitive on this occasion to celebrate one of the Masses "For One Deceased Person" in order to minister to the needs of those who are grieving the loss of this good person.

Other times, there are tragedies (an earthquake, a tsunami, a tornado, etc.) during which many people have died. At times, these tragedies involve the death of friends and relatives in foreign lands. Circumstances prevent the grieving families from attending their funeral Mass. Closer to home, violence on our streets has touched whole communities with the death of innocent people in drive-by shootings or even terrorist attacks. Sometimes, a terrible fire takes the lives of several firefighters or of whole families. On such occasions one of the Masses "For Several Deceased Persons or for All the Dead" may be used to minister to the fears, hurts, and sadness of people touched by these tragedies.

In many cases where you celebrate one of the Masses "For Several Deceased Persons or for All the Dead," there is a pastoral need to affirm the compassion and love of God for grieving people touched by these deaths. In the second Mass of this category, the Collect does a wonderful job of addressing some of these feelings and needs:

> Almighty ever-living God,
> life of all that is mortal and joy of the Saints,
> we humbly pray to you for your servants (N. and N.)
> that, freed from the bonds of mortality,
> they may possess your Kingdom in everlasting glory.

At the same time, there is a group of Masses and Collects in Section IV that at times might fit the circumstances of the celebration even better than the Masses in Part III of "Masses for the Dead."

Part IV contains "Various Prayers for the Dead." Priests and liturgists should become familiar with the various people or groups referenced in this section. I have found the Collect "For a Young Person" effective in ministering to the hurts and anger that people feel over the death of a young person. This Collect says:

> O God, who direct our life in all its moments,
> we humbly entrust to you this your servant, N.,
> whom we mourn as one whose life
> was completed in so short a time;
> grant that he (she) may flourish, for ever young,
> in the happiness of your house.

While the death of a young person often makes us feel sad and angry and finds us questioning our faith (Why did he (she) have to die?), we can begin to address these feelings and questions in selecting a Collect that speaks to the fact that a young person has moved on to experience happiness in God's house.

The Collect "For One Who Suffered a Long Illness" is especially appropriate when a person has been sick, bedridden, or in and out of hospitals for many years. Once again, in situations like these people ask the question: Why me? While there is no completely satisfying answer to this question, the sense in which a sick person can identify themselves with the sufferings of Christ can be the beginning of the type of consolation they need. The Collect says this beautifully:

> O God, who called your servant N.
> to serve you in affliction and sickness,
> grant, we pray,
> that he (she), who followed your Son's example
>   of suffering,
> may also receive the reward of his glory.

We have traditionally taught people to unite their sufferings to those of Christ as a way of making up for one's own sins and the sins of others. In this way, we are taking an intimate part in the suffering of Christ that won for us the gift of salvation.

The Collect "For a Married Couple" reminds us that at times, both husband and wife pass away at the same time or within days of each other's death. The Collect for such a circumstance affirms the goodness of the couple and our hope of eternal life. This Collect says:

> Grant merciful forgiveness, we pray, O Lord,
> to your servants N. and N.,
> that, just as faithful married love
> bound them together in this life,
> so the fullness of your charity
> may unite them for all eternity.

You can almost hear echoes of 1 Corinthians 13:13, which tells us: "And now faith, hope, and love abide, these three; and the greatest of these is love."

Finally, the Collect "For Relatives, Friends, and Bene-factors" reminds us that we should consider celebrating such a Mass, since over the year many good people who fall into one of these categories have died. We need not wait for All Souls' Day to remember them. Especially in communities that have had a great number of deaths, celebrating this particular Mass can continue to heal the sense of loss that many people are experiencing. The Collect says:

> O God, giver of pardon and loving author
> of our salvation,
> grant, we pray you, in your mercy,
> that, through the intercession
> of Blessed Mary, ever-Virgin, and all your Saints,
> the members, friends, and benefactors of
> our community,
> who have passed from this world,
> may attain a share in eternal happiness.

Since this prayer puts into words the thoughts and feelings of many people in the community, I recommend that liturgy committees discuss appropriate times when this Mass could be used to the pastoral benefit of the community.

In summary, the Masses for the Dead contain an extensive group of Masses and Collects that can speak to the whole variety of circumstances under which we celebrate a funeral or memorial Mass. Priests, deacons, bereavement ministers, and liturgy committee members need to familiarize themselves with the Masses and prayers in this section of *The Roman Missal*. I am certain that we will be called upon to celebrate one of these Masses to the spiritual benefit of the people we serve.

Finally, we need to address the question of the use of anniversary Masses and their place in parish life. Masses on the anniversary of the death of a loved one have been an important part of our Catholic tradition. In fact, the intention of many daily Masses is often for a deceased person on their anniversary of death. Yet, in large parishes with only one or two priests, some of these anniversaries need to be grouped together due to the large number of Masses the parish priests are expected to say: daily Mass, Sunday Mass, funerals, weddings, wedding anniversaries, Quinceañeras, etc. We may not be able to offer individual Masses for anniversaries, but we can occasionally schedule a daily Mass "For Relatives, Friends, and Benefactors" of our community. We need to make good use of the many options that this section of *The Roman Missal*, Masses for the Dead, provides for us to minister to the spiritual needs of our people.

QUESTIONS FOR CONTINUED REFLECTION

1. How successful has the implementation of the *Order of Christian Funerals* been in your parishes? What works well? Is there need for improvement?

2. What are the reasons for celebrating a Catholic funeral liturgy? What purpose does the funeral Mass serve?

3. What is the benefit of having a bereavement committee or a liturgy committee assist in the preparation of a funeral Mass?

4. What are the reasons for the successful implementation and acceptance of the *Order of Christian Funerals*? Why do Catholic funerals receive such widespread positive reactions?

5. What has been your experience in attending funerals for baptized and unbaptized children? Have the prayers read at these Masses offered you hope and consolation?

6. What does your parish do to celebrate the anniversaries of the death of loved ones? Is it mainly offering people the chance to have a Mass said for the intention of the deceased person on their anniversary day of death? Has your parish done other types of anniversary Masses?

7. On what occasions have you experienced the celebration of one of the commemorations or memorial Masses found in Part III? Does your parish need to make better use of the Masses in Part III? Give examples from your experience of a time when this would have been helpful.

8. Look at the list of Masses and Collects in Part IV. Which of these Masses or Collects are new to you? Would you like to use them?

9. Would you like to see a Mass scheduled occasionally "For Friends, Relatives, and Benefactors" who have died? How often should this occur?

Chapter 12
The Appendices

The Appendices of *The Roman Missal* have some important materials that you will not find in other parts of the Missal. In this chapter, I will introduce you to some of the helpful materials that you may want to use with your community.

APPENDIX I: VARIOUS CHANTS FOR THE ORDER OF MASS

The first appendix contains a gem that Priest Celebrants, choirs, cantors, musicians, and anyone interested in singing needs to look over. This section contains the various chants that can be used by priests and people during the Mass. Priests need to be encouraged to learn how to sing or chant the appropriate parts of the Mass. Singing adds solemnity and festivity to a celebration.

When would you use the chants in this appendix? Certainly, at choir Masses on Sunday and on special occasions (Christmas Time, Easter Time, Pentecost, Solemnities of the Lord and Mary, and other feasts). If you are the Priest Celebrant, I recommend talking with your music director before Mass so that your chanting of the Preface Dialogue or other parts of the Mass is not a surprise to your musicians.

Appendix I includes additional chants for the Sign of the Cross and the Greeting, Penitential Act, options I and II, the Creed, Our Father, and for the final blessing and dismissal. Also included are the tones for the Prayer of the Faithful and Presidential Prayers (Collect, Prayer over the Offerings, and Prayer after Communion) and the Solemn Blessings, as well as tones for the readings. These latter tones include examples of the full texts of the readings, should these be chanted.

Finally, this first appendix contains a one-page section called the "Announcement of Easter and the Moveable Feasts." The rubrics explain: "On the Epiphany of the Lord, after the singing of the Gospel, a Deacon or cantor, in keeping with an ancient practice of Holy Church, announces from the ambo the moveable feasts of the current year according to this formula."

This tradition could add a sense of the passage of time, marked by significant liturgical celebrations. We often talk about "living" the liturgical year. Using this liturgical "Announcement of Easter and the Moveable Feasts" is one way to encourage people to view these high points of the liturgical year as markers for their progress in the spiritual life. Let's look at this announcement, which is meant to be made on the Solemnity of the Epiphany of the Lord after the proclamation of the Gospel:

> Know, dear brethren, (brothers and sisters,) that, as we
> have rejoiced at the Nativity of our Lord Jesus Christ,
> so by leave of God's mercy we announce to you also
> the joy of his Resurrection, who is our Savior. On the
> . . . day of [February/March] will fall Ash Wednes-
> day, and the beginning of the fast of the most sacred
> Lenten season. On the . . . day of [March/April] you
> will celebrate with joy Easter Day, the Paschal feast of
> our Lord Jesus Christ. On the . . . day of [April/May/
> June] will be the Ascension of our Lord Jesus Christ.
> On the . . . day of [May, June,] the feast of Pentecost.
> On the . . . day of June, the feast of the Most Holy
> Body and Blood of Christ. On the . . . day of [Novem-
> ber, December,], the First Sunday of the Advent of
> our Lord Jesus Christ, to whom is honor and glory for
> ever and ever. Amen.

Quite often parishes meet as a deanery or a grouping of parishes in a geographical area. I recommend that music directors speak to their pastors about the "Announcement of Easter and the Moveable Feasts" and then come to the deanery meeting to share their plans for this special announcement. Especially when beginning something new in the parish, you may want to draw on the experiences of others who have successfully introduced this tradition into their community celebrations on the great Solemnity of the Epiphany of the Lord.

The announcement of "The Nativity of Our Lord Jesus Christ from the Roman Martyrology" concludes Appendix I. As the rubrics note, "this text . . . may be chanted or recited, most appropriately on December 24, during the celebration of the Liturgy of the Hours. It may also be chanted or recited before the beginning of Christmas Mass during the Night." This proclamation traces salvation history and "draws upon Sacred Scripture to declare in a formal way the birth of Christ."

Appendix II: Rite for the Blessing and Sprinkling of Water

In the last edition of *The Sacramentary*, this Rite for the Blessing and Sprinkling of Water was included in the Order of Mass as an alternative to the Penitential Act. Yet in most cases, this rite was only used on the Sundays of Easter Time and days when we recall our Baptism. As a result, the decision was made to place this blessing here in the appendix. This placement in the appendix in no way signifies any lack of importance assigned to this rite.

Let's look at the rubrics:

1. On Sundays, especially in Easter Time, the blessing and sprinkling of water as a memorial of Baptism may take place from time to time in all churches and chapels, even in Masses anticipated on Saturday evenings.

   If this rite is celebrated during Mass, it takes the place of the usual Penitential Act at the beginning of Mass.

2. After the greeting, the Priest stands at his chair and faces
    the people. With a vessel containing the water to be
    blessed before him, he calls upon the people to pray in
    these or similar words:

> Dear brethren (brothers and sisters),
> let us humbly beseech the Lord our God
> to bless this water he has created,
> which will be sprinkled on us
> as a memorial of our Baptism.
> May he help us by his grace
> to remain faithful to the Spirit we have received.

*And after a brief pause for silence, he continues with hands
joined:*

> Almighty ever-living God,
> who willed that through water,
> the fountain of life and the source of purification,
> even souls should be cleansed
> and receive the gift of eternal life;
> be pleased, we pray, to ✚ bless this water,
> by which we seek protection on this your day,
>   O Lord.
> Renew the living spring of your grace within us
> and grant that by this water we may be defended
> from all ills of spirit and body,
> and so approach you with hearts made clean
> and worthily receive your salvation.
> Through Christ our Lord.
> Amen.

Priest Celebrants should notice that the introduction may
be adapted to fit the occasion, since the priest "calls upon the
people to pray in these or similar words." However, the prayer of
blessing of the water does not permit additions or subtractions.
There is also an alternative option provided in the Appendix.

There are two general blessings: a special blessing during Easter Time and a blessing which is designed to be used with the mixing of salt into the water (recalling the command given to the prophet Elisha "to cast salt into water that impure water might be purified"). In all cases, after blessing the water, the rubrics are the same: "Afterwards, taking the aspergillum (water sprinkler), the priest sprinkles himself and the ministers, then the clergy and people, moving through the church, if appropriate."

Very often, I have heard debates about what is the appropriate music to use while the priest sprinkles the congregation. (In cases of a big congregation, the priest may need to have assistants, such as deacons or extraordinary ministers, to help him with the sprinkling of the people.) Sometimes, the Gloria has been sung during the Sprinkling Rite, but the text of the Gloria really does not fit the purpose of the sprinkling rite, which is meant to be a memorial of Baptism. The text of the Gloria never mentions Baptism but is a prayer of praise to our Triune God.

I recommend that choirs learn to sing some of the seven antiphons provided at the end of the Rite for the Blessing and Sprinkling of Water. They are all biblically based. In fact, there is a suggested hymn based on 1 Peter 1:3–5. I am sure that our music publishers will provide suitable settings for these antiphons so that the music accompanying the action of sprinkling fits the purpose of making a memorial of our Baptism.

At the conclusion of the "Rite for the Blessing and Sprinkling of Water," after the singing is over, the Priest is to proclaim this prayer:

> May almighty God cleanse us of our sins,
> and through the celebration of this Eucharist
> make us worthy to share at the table of his Kingdom.
> Amen.

This prayer is similar to the prayer seeking God's forgiveness of our sinfulness proclaimed at the end of the Penitential Rite. According to the rubrics, "when it is prescribed, the hymn Gloria in excelsis (Glory to God in the highest) is sung or said."

APPENDIX III: RITE OF DEPUTING A MINISTER TO DISTRIBUTE HOLY COMMUNION ON A SINGLE OCCASION

This is a helpful rite to have in the Appendices of *The Roman Missal*. Rubric 1 explains that "the Diocesan Bishop has the faculty to permit individual Priests exercising sacred duties to depute a suitable member of the faithful to distribute Holy Communion with them on a single occasion, in cases of real necessity."

If the diocesan Bishop gives this faculty to his priests, they can make use of it when they have a large congregation but insufficient extraordinary ministers in attendance. Sometimes, this situation occurs when celebrating a funeral Mass. They need the assistance of an extraordinary minister in order to facilitate the distribution of Holy Communion in a reasonable amount of time.

If the priest is going to use this faculty, he should make use of the prayer of deputation provided in this Rite. Rubric 2 says: "When one of the faithful is deputed to distribute Communion on a single occasion in such cases, it is fitting that a mandate to do so should be conferred according to the following rite."

Rubric 3 says: "After the Priest Celebrant himself has received the Sacrament in the usual way, the extraordinary minister comes to the altar and stands before the Celebrant, who blesses him or her with these words:

> May the Lord ✝ bless you,
> so that at this Mass you may minister
> the Body and Blood of Christ
> to your brothers and sisters.
> Amen.

APPENDIX IV: RITE OF BLESSING A CHALICE AND A PATEN WITHIN MASS

Another useful text found in the Appendices is the Rite of Blessing a Chalice and a Paten Within Mass. Sometimes, at a funeral Mass, a family will purchased a chalice and paten that they want the priest to use at their loved one's funeral Mass. Often, they inscribe the name of the deceased on the base of the chalice and/or paten for use in future memorial Masses. Sometimes, they donate the chalice and paten to the parish or to the missions.

Rubric number 1 explains the purpose of this rite: "Since the chalice and paten are used for the offering and consecration of the bread and wine and for communion, they are reserved exclusively and permanently for the celebration of the Eucharist, and so become 'sacred vessels.'"

Rubric number 2 further explains why the blessing is celebrated during Mass: "The intention of reserving these vessels exclusively for the celebration of the Eucharist is made manifest before the community of the faithful by a special blessing which it is appropriate to impart during Mass."

Note that rubric number 2 implies the possibility of doing this blessing outside of Mass. For example, a priest might bless the chalice and paten at the wake, where the family may have placed near the casket a special table holding the chalice and paten that they purchased in memory of their loved one.

Rubric number 3 reminds us that "any priest may bless a chalice and paten, provided these vessels have been made according to the norms indicated . . . in the *General Instruction of the Roman Missal*, nos. 327–332." These norms hold that only metal vessels may be used as a chalice or a paten. Glass vessels are no longer permitted to be used and consequently should not be blessed (see also the document *Redemptionis Sacramentum*).

The rite recommends blessing the sacred vessels at the altar immediately after the Universal Prayer (the Prayer of the Faithful) and/or the singing of an appropriate chant. The blessing prayer then follows:

With joy, Lord God,
we place on your altar this chalice and paten
for the celebration of the sacrifice of the new covenant:
may the Body and Blood of your Son,
offered and received by means of these vessels,
make them holy.
Grant, we pray, O Lord,
that, celebrating the unblemished sacrifice,
we may be renewed by your Sacraments on earth
and endowed with your Spirit,
until with the Saints we come to delight in your banquet
in the Kingdom of Heaven.
Glory and honor to you for ever.
All reply: Blessed be God for ever.

Note that the response "Blessed be God for ever" is the same response we make to the prayers over the bread and wine, which follow immediately after this blessing is given. It is at this point that the ministers place the corporal on the altar, the faithful bring up the bread and wine, and the priest puts the offerings on the newly blessed paten and in the newly blessed chalice.

Rubric number 8 recommends that we sing Psalm 116 (115) with a special antiphon: "The chalice of salvation I will raise, / and I will offer a sacrifice of praise." Once again, good communication needs to occur with those responsible for liturgical music, if we are to sing Psalm 116 (115) and its antiphon. When given sufficient time to prepare, I find most musicians are quite willing to accommodate special requests that are appropriate for the occasion.

Rubric number 9 reminds the priest that incensing is possible and can be appropriate: "After the prayer 'With humble spirit,' it is appropriate for the Priest to incense the gifts and the altar." Rubric number 10 recommends the use of the newly blessed chalice to communicate the people: "According to the circumstances of the celebration, it is fitting that the faithful receive the Blood of Christ from the newly blessed chalice."

APPENDIX V: EXAMPLES OF FORMULARIES FOR THE UNIVERSAL PRAYER

Priests and those who prepare the liturgy are frequently looking for sample intentions that they can use when preparing the Prayer of the Faithful (also called the Universal or Bidding Prayer) for Sunday or daily Masses. Let me list the sample formulas and the number of intentions provided in this appendix:

Examples	Number of Intentions
General Formula I	4
General Formula II	8
Advent	8
Christmas Time	4
Lent I	4
Lent II	4
Weekdays of Holy Week	4
Easter Time	4
Ordinary Time I	4
Ordinary Time II	4
Masses for the Dead	10

Of course, these sample petitions all have introductions and concluding prayers that the Priest Celebrant may use. While they usually provide only four sample intercessions, in two cases we have eight intercessions due to the fact that they really have provided us with two sets of four (1 a, 1 b, 2 a, 2 b, 3 a, 3 b, 4 a, 4 b). In the intercessions for the Masses for the Dead, intercession number four has six options depending on the spiritual circumstances of the deceased or the congregation.

Please note that the *General Instruction of the Roman Missal* only recommends four intercessions on each occasion (the Church, the world, those burdened by difficulty, and the local community). Sometimes, we have so many intercessions that they become almost too much to remember. We need to be cautious about having an overabundance of intercessions in our normal experience of worship. There are many places during the course of the Eucharist when we place our intercession before God.

Appendix VI: Sample Invocations for the Penitential Act

Appendix VI includes sample invocations for the Penitential Act. These invocations can be used for option III. The previous edition of *The Sacramentary* contained eight possibilities for option III. Some were more appropriate for particular liturgical times. In the third edition of The Roman Missal, additional options are still provided for those in the dioceses of the United States of America. Rather than printed in the Order of Mass, these options are in the Appendix.

The last section of Appendix VI contains devotional prayers to be said either before or after Mass. Let me first give you a list of the prayers included here, and then let me provide you with a few excerpts from some of the more famous prayers contained in Appendix VI.

Preparation for Mass	Thanksgiving After Mass
Prayer of Saint Ambrose	Prayer of Saint Thomas Aquinas
Prayer of Saint Thomas Aquinas	Prayer to the Most Holy Redeemer

Prayer to the Blessed Virgin Mary	Prayer of Self-Offering
Formula of Intent	Prayer to Our Lord Jesus Christ Crucified
	The Universal Prayer Attributed to Pope Clement XI
	Prayers to the Blessed Virgin Mary

As a a prayer under Preparation for Mass, we have the beautiful Prayer of Saint Ambrose, which begins with these words:

> I draw near, loving Lord Jesus Christ,
> to the table of your most delightful banquet
> in fear and trembling,
> a sinner, presuming not upon my own merits,
> but trusting rather in your goodness and mercy.

This beautiful prayer attempts to place us in the proper mindset for a fruitful celebration of the Holy Eucharist. I encourage you to take a look at it and to use it.

By the inclusion of these prayers in *The Roman Missal*, we are all encouraged to prepare ourselves spiritually prior to celebrating the Eucharist and then to set aside a few moments of prayer after the celebration in order to give thanks to God for the blessings we have received. This used to be a regular part of people's participation in the Eucharist, and restoring such a practice could be a big help to our fruitful participation in the Holy Eucharist.

Let's look at the famous Prayer by Saint Thomas Aquinas in Thanksgiving After Mass:

> I give you thanks,
> Lord, holy Father, almighty and eternal God,

who have been pleased to nourish me,
a sinner and your unworthy servant,
with the precious Body and Blood
of your Son, our Lord Jesus Christ:
this through no merits of mine,
but due solely to the graciousness of your mercy.

I am always struck by the great humility and love embodied in this prayer. Here we have a prayer written by one of the greatest theologians in the history of the Church, yet he does not hesitate to call himself "a sinner and your unworthy servant." Perhaps we can learn a great deal of what is needed to live a spiritual life by slowly meditating on the words of this and similar prayers found in Appendix VI.

I recommend that the prayers found in Appendix VI occasionally be printed in the parish bulletin so that all people might use them, as part of their preparations to celebrate the Eucharistic liturgy with God's people or in their thanksgiving after the celebration of the Holy Eucharist. Often, prayers such as these are printed on the back covers of our annual missals and worship aids or in special appendices in our hymnals.

Like a faithful servant who brings out of his master's storeroom things new and old, this appendix provides devotional prayers that can be a great help to nourishing a healthy spirituality fit for the challenges we face in our daily lives. *The Roman Missal* reminds us that devotional prayers can be helpful supplements to the official liturgical prayers of the Church.

Chapter 13
Conclusion

My goal in this book was to provide an introduction to the third edition of *The Roman Missal* that fairly presents the strengths and weaknesses of the new English translation of the Missal. No translation is perfect, and the new translation will certainly have both admirers and critics.

When you open the cover of *The Roman Missal*, it is good to recall the large number of people involved in developing this new translation:

- The staff and translation committees of the International Commission on English in the Liturgy (ICEL)
- The careful oversight of ICEL's episcopal board, who reviewed every text submitted by ICEL prior to sending it out to their episcopal conferences for their review and recommendations for improvement
- The hard work of the Bishops' Committee on Divine Worship (BCDW) and its many consultants, who assisted the Bishops in developing the final version of the new translation
- The tremendous efforts of numerous episcopal conferences, which met many times to revise and approve the various parts of the Missal prior to submitting a final version to Rome for approval
- The careful involvement of the Vox Clara Committee of Bishops and consultants chosen by the Congregation for Divine Worship and the Discipline of the Sacraments (CDWDS)

- The necessary oversight of the CDWDS to ensure that the translation is accurate and follows contemporary guidelines, especially those contained in *Liturgiam authenticam*

It is important to remember that the new English translation of the third edition of *The Roman Missal* was based on guidelines very different from the ones that inspired the work of the first translators of *The Roman Missal* in the late 1960s and the years thereafter. While it is fair to criticize the inadequacies of the previous translation, we should keep in mind that forty years have passed since the original translation was completed. We now know better than we did in 1970 what we expect in a vernacular translation of the Latin texts of the prayers in *The Roman Missal*.

It is also important to remember that more liberties were taken with the previous English translation of *The Roman Missal* than were taken with the French, German, Italian, and Spanish translations. And so, the English-speaking world is making more adjustments in using the new translation than will other language groups, whose current texts do not require as many changes in order to bring them into accord with contemporary guidelines for translation. For example, the French, German, Italian, and Spanish versions of *The Roman Missal* all translated the response, *et cum spiritu tuo*, as "and with your spirit."

Sometimes, the language of the new translation will appear overly technical. For example, there are many people who object to doctrinal terms such as "consubstantial" and "incarnation." Once again, other language groups kept these terms in their vernacular translation, and so this is mainly a problem among English-speaking communities.

There is a precision in the use of doctrinal terms that does not exist in more colloquial terms. For example, "consubstantial" is a doctrinal term used to define the relationship between the

Father and the Son. "Consubstantial" comes from two words in Latin: *con*, meaning "with," and *substantia*, meaning "substance." The doctrine referred to is the fact that the Son shares "with" the Father the same "substance" or "being." By using the correct doctrinal term we recall the Council of Nicea, which first approved of this term in order to define the relationship between the Father and the Son. Simply translating this word as "one in being" did not adequately convey this connection.

There is no question that the new translation is more accurate, preserves more clearly the biblical and patristic connections to our prayers, and pays greater attention to the poetry, rhythm, and singability of the text. It moves in the direction of developing a special liturgical language for our public prayer, which reflects our inner awareness of our creatureliness when coming into the presence of the God of mystery and awe. While there are improvements in the translation (e.g., we now translate all the words, use the traditional metaphors from the Latin that were often eliminated, and have a text designed to be sung), there are issues that remain unresolved.

One unresolved issue is the length of some sentences, especially in the Prefaces. There is a conflict between being faithful to the Latin text and being faithful to English grammar. The new translation at times uses run-on sentences that contain too many ideas and are thus difficult to understand.

Another unresolved issue is in the selection of words to translate often-used Latin terms. For example, *gaudium* can be translated as "joy" or "gladness." The translators made an effort to follow the guidelines of *Liturgiam authenticam* in providing various ways to translate often-used terms.

Still another unresolved issue is the literal translation of the words in the Institution narrative. For example, some people believe the new translation of *pro multis* in the Consecration of the wine ("It will be shed for you and for many") negates the universal salvific will of Christ. Despite the fact that Pope Benedict XVI himself approved this change and reminded us that "many" is the word chosen by Christ himself in the words of Consecration over the wine, some people still are not convinced. At times, we may have to live with our differences.

Will these changes stand the test of time? Ten years from now, will we look at the disputes over the length of sentences and the selection of words as "much ado about nothing," or will we be petitioning our bishops to seek changes so that the text is more effective in fostering our liturgical prayer? At this point in time, it is impossible to predict what we will be thinking ten years from now.

After all is said and done, the new texts of the third edition of *The Roman Missal* will guide our liturgical prayer for many years to come. These new texts will be the expression and the formation of the spirituality of God's people for a long time. The translators understood this and tried to produce a text that most people could live with.

We need to be grateful to the liturgical leaders who produced the previous translation. It helped us make the transition to a vernacular liturgy a positive experience for many people. While it is easy to point out the flaws in the previous translation, that translation nonetheless mediated our experience of communion with God in many memorable liturgies and special occasions.

The Bishops, priests, and experts who produced the new translation genuinely wanted to produce a text that would be an improvement over the previous edition. They wanted to build on the progress made in developing our liturgical prayer in the previous edition and address some key weaknesses that were in need of correction, especially accuracy and attention to the sources of our prayer tradition. I believe that after using this new translation, most people will be happy with the new translation and see it as a welcome improvement over the previous translation.

In the chapters of this book, I have pointed out many of the new texts that I believe will enrich our faith lives and enliven our liturgical prayer. I invite you to pray that our English-speaking Catholics approach this new translation with an open mind and heart, allowing the Spirit to nourish, to inspire, and to strengthen them in the many years that lie ahead. May the third edition of *The Roman Missal* be an important prayer book that you look forward to using.

Rev. Robert L. Tuzik, PHD